A Kind of Travelling

The Grail Quest Retold

Philippa Craig

Morrigan

*To the Grail people who came each week
through the whole winter to listen to this story.*

Morrigan
*Killala
County Mayo
Ireland*

©2001 The Grail Society

ISBN 0 907677 63 0

Published by Morrigan in association with
Grail Publications
*Waxwell Lane
Pinner
Middlesex
UK*

Design & Origination by Melt Design, Dublin.
Printed in Ireland by Techman

*All rights reserved. No part of this publication may be copied,
reproduced or transmitted in any form or by any means,
without the permission of the copyright owner.*

Contents

Introduction		iv
People in the Story		vi
Chapter 1	The Prophecies of Merlin	1
Chapter 2	The Rowan Tree	11
Chapter 3	Towards the Sea	23
Chapter 4	The Nine Stars in the Sky	31
Chapter 5	The Dark Powers	41
Chapter 6	A Kind of Knowledge	53
Chapter 7	The Ship from the North	65
Chapter 8	The Lonely Season	77
Chapter 9	The Meeting Place	89
Chapter 10	In the Eye of the Sun	99
Chapter 11	The Winter World	111
Bibliography		123
The Grail Society		124

The motif at the chapter headings shows a seal of the Templar Knights. The author of The Quest of the Holy Grail may have had them in mind when he recreated the story. The Templars were vowed to the protection of pilgrims and of the Holy Places in Jerusalem. In the springtime of their Order, these men were a far cry from the self-seeking ambitious knights of the age. The Templar seal expresses the poverty and loyalty of its members by showing two knights sharing the same horse.

Introduction

The Quest of the Grail is only one of a vast collection of Arthurian tales which spread across Europe in the 13th century. These tales grew out of earlier legends, folk lore, wonder-tales and so-called histories. Since the stories were recited, rather than read, they changed with each re-telling, according to the intentions and creativity of whoever told them.

Perhaps the most famous of these story tellers was Chrétien de Troyes who produced a whole series of Arthurian poems for recital in the household of his patron, Philip of Alsace, Duke of Flanders. One of these poems is "Parcival, the Story of the Grail", Unfortunately, before he could finish this huge work of more than 9000 lines Chrétien died and soon afterwards other hands set out to complete it, to recast it.

In Chrétien's poem Parcival, the hero, is resting during his travels. He is sitting at table, when he sees a procession pass through the room. Leading it is a woman who holds a dish, a gold, bejewelled vessel which Chrétien calls a "grail". It is obvious that this grail is a mysterious object, though Chrétien does not give it any special religious significance. Yet within ten years of his death it had acquired the aura of an incomparable Christian relic.

Robert de Boron, a French knight, retold the story and in doing so he transformed the grail into the holy Grail. This, he said, was the very dish which Christ had used at the Last Supper, and which Joseph of Arimathea had brought to Britain, where, it was now hidden.

In all subsequent versions the Grail is described as something holy beyond words, a treasure waiting to be found. Whether the essence of the grail lay in the vessel itself, in its emptiness, in its contents, or in its hiddenness, is never stated. Nor are its strange powers of bringing blessing as well as calamity ever reconciled. These ambiguities remain to make the Quest the most mysterious of all the Arthurian stories.

If Robert de Boron had altered Chrétien's poem, so in turn his version was retold still more radically when The Quest of the Holy Grail appeared around 1220. Nobody knows who wrote it but it is clear that the author, though certainly not a monk himself, was familiar with the life and spirituality of the Cistercians. He was probably a scribe or copyist in some Cistercian monastery.

This man took the familiar story and recreated it on a different plane. He turned the knights' search for the hidden Grail into what he called "a search into the deep mysteries of God."

This gave him an immediate problem. The characters and exploits of Parcival, Lancelot and the rest were all firmly fixed in the public imagination. They were, all of them, too flawed to succeed in such a search. So the writer discarded Parcival and Lancelot as heroes and created a completely new character, a truly single-hearted knight and called him Galahad.

It is likely that in Galahad and his companions he saw images of the life and strivings of the Knights Templar in Jerusalem, the military order which had links with the Cistercians and for whom St Bernard had drawn up a rule of life. And since these fictional knights were to be men truly searching for God, the author scattered throughout the story Cistercian monasteries and monks whose task it was to give counsel and encouragement for the journey. In a word, the new version made the familiar adventure story into a sort of Pilgrim's Progress, a guide to individual Christian response, a guide specifically for lay people.

It is not possible to know how contemporary readers or listeners responded to this new version. When the Quest was written the crusades had been going on sporadically for a hundred years and the return from Jerusalem of knights, clerics, merchants and plain adventurers was creating great changes in aspirations and attitudes. The west was gaining new knowledge of medicine, mathematics and the rudiments of science. Theology was growing into rival schools, towns and social structures were developing. Cathedrals were being built, giving rise to new art forms and architecture. The externals of Christian faith were taking on new colour and beauty though this was not true of the lay folk's religious world. Theirs was a world of ignorance, incomprehension and the lowest of expectations.

Nowhere is this shown more clearly than in the position of laymen and women in the Christian liturgy. Since virtually no lay people ever saw what happened in the Mass, and the Church's penitential discipline made the reception of the Eucharist almost impossible for ordinary men and women, it is not surprising that they were no more than onlookers.

A few years before The Quest was written the Archbishop of Paris had ruled that the host must be shown to the people during Mass. This was a belated effort to give them some part in the liturgy but as the practice spread it gave rise to fantasies and superstitions, even to real fear. It also caused disagreement between clergy who thought the practice irreverent and those who considered it a great revelation. The Cistercian author shows the knights present at a number of Masses or liturgies, and in most of them this conflict and confusion of ideas is reflected.

It is significant that The Quest of the Holy Grail apparently never received any official approbation from the Church as a spiritual guide for lay people. Perhaps it was its strange blending of Christian teaching with magic, apparitions, and relations with the natural world that made it suspect. Equally though, the book was never denounced. Today it can be seen as one person's attempt to bring men and women closer to God through telling them a story.

People in the Story

Arthur	Legendary king of Britain, ruler of an empire of thirty kingdoms, and head of the famous company of Knights of the Round Table.
Guinevere	Arthur's queen, beautiful daughter of the king of Cornwall, she was fated to bring disaster on the fellowship of knights.
Merlin	An enigmatic unpredictable figure from West Wales; a sorcerer who counselled the king up to the time of his marriage with Guinevere.
Lancelot	Arthur's right hand, the most famous and respected knight in the whole company.
Hector	Lancelot's brother, a less admirable figure, whose quest brought him little in return for his labours.
Galahad	Lancelot's son, youngest of all the knights who went on the Grail quest.
Parcival	A Welsh youth totally ignorant of courtly ways, who had found his path to Arthur's court from the remotest part of Snowdonia.
Bors	Contemporary of Arthur, a loyal fighter in all his wars. A close friend of Arthur and Guinevere.
Lionel	Brother of Bors. While on the quest he turned against Bors and almost destroyed him.
Gawain	Nephew of King Arthur and eldest of the four sons of Lot, king of Orkney. It was he who instigated the quest. He was also the first knight to withdraw from it.
Mordred	Brother of Gawain. An ambitious, violent man who, when the quest was over, set out to destroy Arthur and to capture his kingdom.
Dindrane	Older sister to Parcival, she had not been brought up in his solitude but in touch with the world of knighthood. She joined Bors, Parcival and Galahad on their quest for the Grail.
Nescien	A wandering preacher who led Galahad to Arthur's court and thus signalled the beginning of the Grail quest.
King Pelles	Galahad's grandfather, lord of Castle Carbonek where the Grail was hidden, and where Galahad had spent his earliest years.
King Pellam	Galahad's great-grandfather, the sick old man who lived on in Carbonek, "the maimed king" who had brought calamity on himself and the whole of his kingdom.

CHAPTER 1

The Prophecies of Merlin

No sooner has the unknown knight Galahad arrived at Arthur's court at Whitsun than the Grail vessel reveals itself briefly in the midst of the festivities. This mysterious apparition, veiled from their sight, triggers off the knights' resolve to go in search of it, to see it clearly, to understand its significance. Little do they realise how lengthy and demanding the journey will be for each of them.

No one of King Arthur's knights in Camelot knew much about his counsellor Merlin, only that the old man had been with the King longer than anyone could remember. Knights, squires and servants all went in a certain fear of him, for Merlin had powers which no one could explain.

Rumour had it that he could change his human shape and become a deer, a raven, a standing stone, or even become invisible. Wherever Merlin went people discussed him. Some said 'His father was one of those spirits that live between the earth and the moon; half-human creatures that roam the world and sometimes mate with women. He is a demon in disguise.'

But others denied this and said 'No, he is a Christian man. Otherwise, would the King be guided by him?'

So they did not know what to believe.

Arthur had none of these doubts. He knew that Merlin was his true and constant counsellor, his life-long protector. Even before Arthur was born, Merlin had seen his future glory. A star shaped like a dragon appeared in the sky one winter's night, and Merlin interpreted it to Uther, the king who ruled in those days.

'That dragon star is you' he said, 'so you must now call yourself Uther Pendragon. That great beam of light which springs from the star is your son Arthur. He will be a great man and build a brotherhood of knights, and rule over many kingdoms.'

As time passed, all of this came true and Arthur embarked on nothing without Merlin's counsel.

There was only one occasion when Arthur rejected Merlin's words; this was when he chose the Cornish princess Guinevere to be his wife.

'She is the fairest lady I could ever find' said Arthur.

'I know about her' Merlin answered, 'and what you say is true as to her beauty. Still, I think she is not meant for you.' Later, he spoke secretly to Arthur, saying: 'You should not take Guinevere as your wife. The time will

1

come when she will love another man and betray you, and bring grief and trouble on you all.'

But Arthur had made up his mind. When Merlin saw that his warning was unheeded, he said:

'Well, where your heart points, there you will go. I shall give you no more warnings.'

After this, Arthur sent Merlin to Cornwall as his ambassador. With him went two of the King's most loyal knights, Bors and Lionel; two brothers who had fought at Arthur's side in all his wars. They brought Guinevere back with great solemnity. She rode in the midst of a troop of Cornish lords, each one of them in black armour, each holding a white pennant on which the Cornish chough was painted: fifty black birds with red beaks and red claws.

Once Arthur and Guinevere were married at St. Stephen's church in Winchester, Merlin went away for a time to Avalon to continue his study of the healing power of stones.

On his return he realised that some of Arthur's knights were quarrelling among themselves for greater honour in the King's eyes. This grieved Merlin and he said 'You are all here as brothers and equals. Remember the customs of this fellowship of yours: it is to support and defend the King and one another; to take care of poor men, women, widows and orphans; and to keep peace in the land. You are not here for your own advantage.'

After this, he got carpenters to make a great round table. Built of wood and stone, it took up nearly the whole of the castle hall. Around the table were a hundred and forty seats, each one with the name of a knight written on it. As they sat thus in a circle, all were shown to be equal as Merlin had intended. He said 'This table is an image of the roundness of the earth and the movement of the planets. In these heavenly spheres we see the stars and many things besides to tell us of future happenings.'

It was soon noticed that three of the seats remained empty and without names. The knights asked Merlin what this meant. He said:

'They are there for three knights who will join your fellowship. One of them will come next Whitsun. He is called Lancelot of the Lake because he has lived beside the lake in Avalon. The second seat is kept for Parcival who will come from Wales, though it will be fifteen years or more before he comes. And the third will be for Galahad. He will come soon after that, though no one knows the day. When he comes, strange things will happen and secrets will be revealed, and the lives of all of you will be touched, for good or ill.'

They did not understand and were not bold enough to question him, except for Bors who asked: 'Tell us about these secrets and strange events.' Merlin said:

'They concern the Grail. You all know that the Grail is the dish used at Christ's last supper with his friends, and that Joseph of Arimathea brought it here; that his family has guarded it ever since, though where it is housed no one knows.'

The Prophecies of Merlin

There was a murmur of agreement; the story was common knowledge. Merlin went on:

'Sometimes, the Grail leaves its hiding place and shows itself to people, though no one ever sees it plainly. It is always concealed, and it vanishes away again. This knight Galahad will go in search of it.'

This impressed his audience, who said:

'For a man like that, a special seat ought to be made.'

'That I will do' Merlin told them. Then by magic he made these warning words write themselves on the wooden chair:

THIS IS THE SEAT OF DANGER. IT IS MEANT FOR THE ONE WHO COMES. LET ANYONE ELSE USE IT AT HIS PERIL.

That year passed, and the following Whitsun Lancelot came from Avalon to Camelot where he was made a knight. By this time Merlin considered that his work for the King was finished, so he left the court secretly and went away to a cave in the mountains where he could spend his time studying the movements of the stars. He knew that Lancelot was the knight who would betray Arthur with Queen Guinevere, but he kept his knowledge to himself.

A further sixteen years went by, and then Parcival appeared from the Snow Mountains of Wales. His arrival had been so bizarre that knights spoke of it years afterwards. For he arrived on a shaggy mountain pony and rode straight to Arthur and Guinevere saying:

'Make me a knight, sir.' Not humbly at all, but as though it were his due.

A murmur ran round the assembly, as men asked:

'Who is this scarecrow? What right has he to speak?'

Indeed, he hardly looked like a candidate for knighthood, for he wore a coarse canvas shirt and a leather jacket. His legs were bare and his feet protected by home-made leather boots tied together with straps. He was small and agile and not at all subdued by the disapproval in the hall. He said:

'I am Parcival, the Welsh man.'

Some of the knights began to laugh, and Arthur grew angry when he heard them. He said severely:

'This young man may well turn out to be a good knight if he is ready to learn what we can teach him.'

So Parcival remained and when he had learned enough Arthur knighted him, to the disapproval of the other knights who still thought of him as unsuitable, as an overconfident ignoramus.

A year after Parcival became a knight, two strange events took place at Camelot.

The first was the appearance of a totally unknown woman who rode into the great hall where the knights sat at table. She dismounted and approached Arthur and Guinevere with great composure. She wanted a favour from the King, she said.

'May Lancelot go with me into the forest? I have a mission there and it needs his presence.'

Everyone stared at her with surprise and wondered who she could be, and how she had been able to enter into the castle unhindered. The King, too, was taken aback, but he agreed to her request.

She and Lancelot then rode away among the trees, down a green lane that descended into a valley. Here they halted before the gates of a Cistercian nunnery, where they were made welcome. Indeed, they received a double welcome for they found Bors and his brother Lionel there in the guest quarters, on their way back to Camelot for the Whitsun gathering.

Presently, three nuns presented themselves and asked Lancelot to knight a youth who had recently been brought to them.

'He is certainly fit to become a knight' they told him.

He fell in with their wishes, only stipulating that this must be the youth's own choice. Once this was determined, he made the tall young man a knight; he had no idea of his identity.

'May God make you a good man and a faithful knight' he said, and rode back alone to the Castle.

The second strange happening was the appearance of a great stone floating on the river beside the Castle. The whole company hastened to the riverside to see the great block of red marble in the water, and driven into its heart a sword. Looking close, they could see letters of gold written on the hilt. They read:

NO ONE SHALL TAKE ME OUT OF THIS STONE
EXCEPT THE ONE BY WHOSE SIDE I OUGHT TO HANG.

They were all amazed.

'Whose sword can it be?' they asked each other. 'And how can a stone float? What sort of omen is this?'

None of them knew that they were looking at Merlin's work. He had taken a sword from one of Arthur's knights some twenty years earlier; by magic he had thrust it into the stone, and by the same magic he had made it float to Camelot.

Having examined the stone, Arthur said to Lancelot who had now returned: 'You are certainly the best knight among us, so take out the sword.'

Lancelot knew that he was certainly not the best knight, so he made excuse:

'That sword is not meant for me,' he said. 'I am sure of it. I dare not try to take it out.'

His face grew sombre, and he said:

'That sword has some strange power within it. If the wrong man tries to draw it, he will suffer for his action. Who knows where that sword was forged, or who was the swordsmith?"

The Prophecies of Merlin

Then Arthur urged Gawain his nephew to try. He obeyed but could not shift the sword an inch, though he exerted all his strength and grew scarlet in the face with his efforts.

'You will regret this' Lancelot told him. 'Believe me, Gawain, one day that very blade will cut you down, and you will remember it as long as you live.'

The next day being Whit Sunday, the fellowship took their places at the Round Table. As they ended their meal, all the doors and windows suddenly swung shut of their own accord, yet the hall remained full of light.

'What can this mean?' they said to one another uneasily.

As they were speaking, an old man dressed as a priest came in with a tall young man at his side. The youth wore a chain-mail shirt covered with a red linen surcoat. He had neither sword nor shield, only a scabbard hanging by his side on a leather strap. He looked round and greeted the assembled knights, and Lancelot immediately recognised him as the youth he had knighted the day before.

Then the old man said to Arthur 'Sir, I am Nescien the hermit. I bring you this young knight who is the descendant of kings and of the family of Joseph of Arimathea. Through him, the enchantment that lies on this land will be lifted, kings will be healed, the land will become green again and many secrets will be revealed.'

At this, the young man went straight to the empty seat at the Round Table. The writing on it had miraculously changed, and now the letters said:

THIS IS THE SEAT OF GALAHAD, THE GREAT PRINCE.

So Galahad sat down on it, and they all stared at him in wonder.

Lionel said to Bors:

'This is surely the one Merlin spoke about, for no one else has ever dared to sit in that seat.'

Bors answered secretly:

'If he is the one, then he will bring great changes to the fellowship.'

Arthur took the new arrival by the hand and showed him every honour. And before long, the whole Castle rang as people speculated on Galahad's arrival. Even the Queen and her attendants were caught up in the excitement.

'Where does he come from? Does anyone know him?'

'He has been staying with Nescien, the old hermit who brought him.'

'He is a handsome man; he is taller than Lancelot.'

'He looks like Lancelot. Could he be related?'

'They say he is the grandson of King Pelles of Carbonek.'

When Guinevere heard all this, she said bitterly to her ladies:

'I know who he is: I can well believe that he is that boy born to Elaine, the daughter of King Pelles, after she ensnared Lancelot by a magic trick. Yes, this is certainly Lancelot's son who has come here to Camelot.'

Arthur said to Galahad again:

'You are welcome among us. I believe that you are the one Merlin spoke of, the one we wait for.'

After this, he took him down to the river's edge and showed him the stone and the sword, saying 'No one can take it out, though many have tried.'

'I will take it out' said Galahad. 'That is why I have no sword with me, but only a scabbard.'

He took the hilt in his hand and drew it out easily. Every knight saw this happen; and Guinevere, too, for she had taken her ladies down to the river bank. She was full of curiosity, and looked hard at this son of Lancelot's.

'All I need now is a shield.' said Galahad.

'Since God sent you this sword,' said Arthur, 'surely he will send you a shield as well.'

The King was quite overcome by what he had seen, for in his own youth he had drawn a sword out of a great stone in the churchyard of St. Paul's church in London. He alone had been able to draw it, and by this act had shown himself the rightful king. Now Galahad had performed the same act and proved himself the knight of whom Merlin had spoken.

As Arthur was considering all this, the horsewoman they had seen the previous day rode up and greeted the king and queen.

'Is Sir Lancelot here?' she asked, and when he came forward she began to weep, saying:

'Oh, Lancelot! Today your fortunes are changed. Once you were the best knight of all, but today another has that place since you were afraid to draw that sword out of the stone.'

Then the woman turned to Arthur:

'Today' she told him, 'you will receive the greatest honour any king has ever known. This very day the Grail will come into your house, and you and all your fellowship will be fed and strengthened by it.'

Then she rode swiftly away, and once again the knights wondered who she was and how she came by this knowledge.

As for Arthur, he was jubilant.

'We are seeing marvellous things today' he cried, 'and this is only the beginning! So let us have a tournament on the river meadow. Let everyone celebrate, so they will remember this day in years to come.'

Before long the meadow was decked with pennants and flags, and the knights set about their mock battles, sometimes in single combat, sometimes one group against another. They used lances, swords and even axes, and there were many blows and bruises given, even though the tournament weapons were blunted for the occasion.

Galahad had fought without a shield yet he was not harmed, and he even managed to unhorse many of his opponents. Everybody wondered at his skill, especially Guinevere and her ladies who sat and watched and applauded the victors.

When evening came, the herald declared the tournament to be over and Arthur led Galahad back into the castle.

Soon afterwards, they all took their seats at the table. Without any warning, there came a tremendous roll of thunder, followed by a ray of brilliant white light that made a mockery of the many candles burning in the hall. Then there was total silence. The knights sat motionless, rigid with expectancy.

In that silence, the Grail vessel appeared in the beam of light. Hidden within a shining cloth, it floated above the table of its own volition, sending out a wonderful aroma of every sort of herb and spice. Moreover, as it moved, each knight found before him on the table his favourite food.

When everyone had been served, the light faded and the Grail vanished with it. No hand had supported it; no one knew where it had gone.

They all sat in silence for a time, quite bemused. Then Arthur's nephew Gawain got to his feet. The others looked at him with expectation. He was a man of influence among them, a proud prince from the Orkney Islands, masterful and fierce. He said:

'Tonight the Grail has been with us. It showed itself to us but only in a hidden way. I want to know more; I want to discover where it is housed. I have made up my mind: I shall go in search of it. No matter how long it takes, I will not return until I have found it and seen it plainly.'

He spoke with such determination that other knights stood up and began to make similar promises, and eventually all the hundred and forty men undertook the search for it.

Next day the King's chaplain asked them to ratify their promises, so they went in a group to the castle chapel where the priest brought out a book of the gospels and a blessed silver bell. They could place their hand on either to take the oath.

Before Gawain could begin, Bademagus one of the Scots lords intervened, suggesting that Galahad should be the first.

'It is he who sat in the Seat of Danger and we should give him precedence.'

So Galahad took the oath first, then Lancelot who was Arthur's right hand, then Gawain, Bors, Lionel and Parcival; and after them the rest of the company.

Now as Arthur watched the ceremony his feelings began to change and his heart grew heavy. He said within himself:

'Who will defend Camelot and the kingdom if the whole fellowship is absent? How many of the knights will never come back from this quest?'

His anxiety increased. He called for Gawain and said:

'You have done me a great disservice, nephew. Because of your words, everyone will go on this search and who knows when you will come back.'

Gawain said:

'We have gone on many journeys before this and succeeded. We shall all return in safety, have no fear.'

But the King then appealed to Lancelot, saying:

'I wish you were not leaving me. God knows what you may meet on the journey; every sort of danger and deceit. And how long will you be away? It is an unknown path you are taking. I should never have agreed to let you go.'

Again they both said:

'We cannot go back on our promises.'

When the King realised that they were not to be moved, he left them and spent the whole night wandering through Camelot, sleepless, sad, deeply disturbed.

Arthur's gloom was infectious, and next day many ladies and wives in the castle wept too, at the thought of what would happen; of their being left alone with few defences and no loved ones. Then one of the young knights thought he had found a solution.

'Let us all go together' he cried out, 'wives and friends, loved ones and ladies!'

But before they could applaud this solution, the knights heard the voice of the old man who had brought Galahad to Camelot. He called for silence, raised his right hand like a prophet and cried:

'None of you may take wife, friend or lover with you. Each one of you must go alone on this journey.'

The young knight was angered by these words, and turned to the assembly saying:

'Who is this man, to tell us what to do?'

Those around him silenced him. Then Galahad put his hand on the old man's shoulder and said:

'Sir, this is Nescien, the servant of God. He has the right to speak to us.'

Nescien ignored the young knight and fixed his eyes on Gawain. He said again:

'Each of you must make your own way; you must go alone. This quest is no search for money or fame or power. It is a journey into the deep mysteries of God. Do not underestimate it.'

'What deep mysteries are these?' said Gawain impatiently.

Nescien told him:

'They are to do with God's presence in the world, and the longing he has given us to find him.'

Now while Arthur was grieving at the knights' departure, Queen Guinevere was full of anger at the thought of Lancelot's leaving her. She refused to see anyone, locked herself in her room, flung herself down on her bed and wept without restraint. Guinevere thought only of Lancelot. For since he had come to Arthur's court twenty years ago, he and Guinevere had been secret lovers, as Merlin had foreseen.

When Lancelot himself went to make his farewells, she dismissed him with furious tears.

'Have you no thought of me, left all alone in this place?' she demanded. 'How long will you be absent? Am I to spend my time embroidering copes for bishops, or playing chess, or gossiping with the ladies here, or riding in the woods with the King?'

The Prophecies of Merlin

He was silent and she said:

'I see that you have no love or loyalty for me, or you would stay here. So go on this quest which you prefer to me.'

Bors, who was Lancelot's greatest friend, saw his unhappiness. He went straight to the Queen, whom he had known for twenty years, and said plainly:

'Madam, stop this weeping and complaining. You are for ever seeing dangers and slights where none exist. Let Lancelot go and give him your blessing.'

But Guinevere grew even angrier. She wept aloud and beat her hands on the table in front of her.

'That false knight Lancelot!' she cried. 'If he leaves me now, let him never come back into my sight!'

Next morning she looked down fiercely from the window of her tower, having dismissed her ladies and attendants. In the courtyard below, the knights were gathering the horses led in by their squires, and examining their spears and shields.

Guinevere caught sight of Lancelot in the midst of a group clustered round him: his brother Hector, Gawain and his young brothers from the Orkneys, and Bademagus, the Scots lord. She noticed that Bors and his brother Lionel stood together somewhat apart, deep in conversation. Presently they set to examining their gear. Both were experienced travellers and had no thought of leaving things to chance. In their saddlebags they had iron rations for themselves and their horses, as well as horse-picks, awls, leather strips, needles and thread for mending harness, sharp knives and files; to say nothing of strips of linen for bandages, should need arise.

The departure was a sad occasion, and not only for the King and Queen. All the people in the town, rich and poor, farmers and merchants, followed the knights, as did the remaining defenders of the castle, a few old knights, veterans of many wars. The knights were fully armed with lances, shields and swords; many had hooked on the face-guards of their helmets so no one could discern their feelings as they said goodbye. Yet some of them seemed happy and excited. Certainly Parcival was not cast down, waving his red shield with its white springing stag and singing aloud as he did so.

King Arthur rode with his knights through Camelot, over the meadow and over the river to the edge of the forest. There were few paths or tracks. The forest was wild and frightening, full of hidden dangers. They rode on in the half light, in the green twilight of the trees. Presently, the King left them and rode away in deep unhappiness and apprehension.

The knights said goodbye to their friends. They remembered what Nescien, the wandering preacher had said: 'This is a journey for each one of you. Each of you must find your own path.'

So they said to each other 'It would be cowardly if we all stayed together in one group.'

After that, each knight rode off alone into the dark forest.

A Kind of Travelling

CHAPTER 2

The Rowan Tree

Despite the knights' firm intention to ride separately, it proves impossible since they inevitably meet up with one another by chance and learn how their comrades are faring. Gawain and Hector join forces with the intention of making Galahad the third member of their company, convinced that he will bring them more success than they have met so far. These hopes are disappointed. And whereas Galahad's earliest endeavours on the quest are all in defence of helpless people, Gawain and Hector bring violence and destruction along every path they ride.

When the feast of Michaelmas came round the knights had been on their quest for four months or more, and already their numbers had dwindled. Sickness, capture by enemies, death, lack of resolve, disillusionment had all taken their toll.

Among those remaining on the quest the first excitement had subsided, and this was particularly true of Gawain who had instigated the search and swept the other knights along on his enthusiasm.

To begin with, he had ridden confidently into the forest. He was used to success, for not only was he one of Arthur's nephews, he was also prince of the three kingdoms of Denmark, Norway and the Orkney Isles. But as spring became summer and then autumn, he began to wonder why everything seemed exactly as it always had been. So far as excitement went he might have been on a routine law-enforcement mission, rather than a search for a hidden treasure which only a few chosen knights could expect to find.

By day he rode through woodland and clearings beside small rivers, and through poor villages where he saw few people. By night he slept in the guest-house of one monastery or another. Here he always asked his fellow guests if there was news of any strange or unexpected happening in the neighbourhood. But they seldom had anything to tell him, being more concerned about the weather than anything else.

'This will be a ruinous year' said the guest house monk. 'There are no beech nuts on the trees, and hardly any acorns either; no food for pigs at all.'

'Worse than that', said a merchant, 'Look at the market in the churchyard here – hardly any beans or peas for sale. What's going to happen when the real cold weather comes?'

'The birds are coming here already' said the monk. 'They know all about the weather, coming from the north as they do. I have seen the geese myself, arrows of them overhead day after day all last week. They are much too early. That might be a sign for you, sir' he said to Gawain.

But Gawain merely nodded; such talk meant nothing to him.

Next day, he rode away in silent discontent.

A couple of weeks later he met other knights whose search had been no more exciting than his own, and when he fell in with Lancelot's brother Hector, he found a man even more disappointed than himself.

They met at a ferry over a crossing. Rain was sweeping over the river in long drifts, and their surcoats streamed with water as they waited for the ferryman to bring the pontoon from the other bank.

Hector said 'I've ridden all this time, west and north, over miserable hills and marshes and I must have met at least twenty knights who feel the same as we do. They've found nothing, they've lost heart and they don't know which road to take.'

'Is there any news of Galahad?' Gawain asked. His immediate wish was to find him and stay in his company, for that prospect might offer some hope of success. Hector shook his head.

'No one has met up with him, so far as I know' he said. 'He's vanished – and so have Lancelot and Bors as well.'

Once on the far side of the river, Hector and Gawain decided to ride together since that might bring them better luck. They rode away into the densest part of the forest where the tree-tops made a dark dripping roof above them, and the track beneath the trees was dank and thick with fallen leaves.

Meanwhile, miles away, Galahad was asking hospitality in a Cistercian monastery. To his surprise he found two other knights already settled there, one being Bademagus, the Scots lord. Soon all three of them were sitting together among the apple trees in the monastery orchard, and when they had each recounted the story of his quest so far, Bademagus said:

'This abbey has a great treasure but few people know about it because the monks don't want it to be seen.'

'What is it, then? Some relic of a saint? Something wonderful brought back from Jerusalem?'

'More than that; they say it is an ancient shield from the days of Joseph of Arimathea. The story is that if anyone tries to take it away, some evil will fall on him.'

'Do you believe it?'

'No' said Bademagus. 'I don't, and what is more I'm going to take it away myself tomorrow, so you can both see what the legend is worth.'

Next day he spoke with the abbot, asking to be shown the shield. Inspecting it closely, he found that it was certainly ancient, battered and strained with use. It was made of layers of wood and leather, edged with a metal rim. The shield had been painted white and at the centre someone had painted a rough red cross. Bademagus took the shield and, despite the protests of the abbot, slung it on his back and hastened away from the monastery, taking his Danish squire Melias with him. They rode for several miles and came to the base of a grassy hill.

All at once a threatening figure loomed on the hilltop, a knight on a tall grey horse with no markings to identify him; his shield, his surcoat, his lance, his armour all as white as wood ash. He gave a great shout and rode fiercely towards them.

It was now that Bademagus was punished for his reckless theft of the shield, for though he defended himself with vigour his efforts laid him open to a tremendous sword-stroke that cut through his chain-mail, tore him from the saddle and left him bleeding into the grass.

'Take that shield away from him and give it to me!' the knight shouted, and the shocked squire Melias hastened to obey him.

The knight said to Melias: 'This shield is meant for Galahad, and for no one else. Take it back to the abbey and give it to the abbot. Tell Galahad that it will keep him safe no matter what the danger. And if Galahad meets me tomorrow in this place, I will tell him the story of the shield.'

Presently Galahad saw the squire return, holding the wounded Bademagus before him on his horse. He ran to give assistance, calling for the infirmarian of the abbey.

It looked as though Bademagus would die, for his wound was gaping and bloody, but the monk-doctor had no such fears; in fact, he had little sympathy for Bademagus.

'He brought this on himself' he said dourly. 'He has no respect for holy things. Anyway, no doubt he will live. I will treat him with woundwort. If you crush the leaves and put a poultice on the bark of a dying tree, it will recover; so I suppose it will heal him, too.'

After Bademagus had been settled in a quiet room, and Melias had recounted what had happened, the abbot sent for Galahad and put the shield into his keeping. It was to serve him well, but as time passed it grew ever more splintered, bruised and frayed.

When he learned that his lord would have to remain in the abbey for some weeks, the squire Melias begged to be allowed to ride with Galahad. Bademagus got so tired of Melias' repeated requests that he gave permission provided Galahad agreed. Because of the squire's inexperience Galahad was reluctant to take him as his squire, but in the end he agreed. Next day, they left the abbey together and rode to the green hill where the knight was waiting for them.

'Follow me' he said, 'and I will tell you all you ought to know.'

He led them down the hill and along a hollow lane overhung with hazel trees.

Melias rode behind, listening as the knight told Galahad how Joseph of Arimathea and his sons had been forced to leave their home near Jerusalem and to travel westwards, where they had settled in a town called Sarras.

'Have you heard of Joseph of Arimathea?' he asked.

Galahad said 'I know that he came to Britain to trade for tin and copper.'

'That is true,' said the knight, 'and that is why he settled here, because he was familiar with Cornwall and the Summerlands. But Joseph had to face such hostility in this country that he and all his family were imprisoned. This came to the ears of King Mordrain of Sarras who had been Joseph's great friend and protector. He sailed here from Sarras with his army and set Joseph free. Then he settled here as well.'

The knight drew up his horse and looked around him at the forest they were now entering. Then he said: 'Have you ever been to the holy shrine in Glastonbury?'

'Why, yes' said Galahad, surprised. 'The place which people call Avalon, where the great apple orchards were? I have seen the tombs of St. David and St. Patrick there. It is a great abbey.'

'It is a holy place' said the knight, 'because it was there that Joseph built the first Christian church in this land.'

'Joseph died,' he continued 'and his son Josephus fell ill and was on his death-bed, but King Mordrain was still alive. He asked the dying Josephus for a relic, a remembrance. After some thought Josephus remembered the white shield he had given Mordrain years before. The shield was brought to him, and on the white surface he painted a red cross using his own blood. "This colour will never fade" he told Mordrain, "and when you, too, come to die, see that the shield is put in a monastery to await the day when my last descendant will come to claim it."'

The knight said to Galahad 'With your arrival that day has come.'

Then he said goodbye and rode away down a shadowed track.

Galahad and Melias continued on for a week or more, crossing heathland and low hills, passing little villages where women and children were working together gathering fallen wood and nuts from the hazel trees.

Soon they came to the beginning of an ancient forest, many of the trees gnarled and ruined. Two tracks lay ahead, between them a notice on a wooden post. It read:

TAKE THE RIGHT PATH AND YOU WILL REACH YOUR JOURNEY'S END, THOUGH NOT BY YOUR OWN STRENGTH. TAKE THE LEFT PATH AND YOU WILL ONLY WIN THROUGH IF YOUR OWN STRENGTH IS SUFFICIENT.

'Let me take the left path!' cried Melias. 'I am strong enough for that!'

Galahad was dubious.

'You have no experience' he said. 'Keep to the right path, as any sensible man would do.'

But Melias went on urging him, refusing to be dissuaded, so Galahad wasted no time in rebuking him but let him have his way.

The Rowan Tree

The first surprising thing that Melias came upon was a shelter built of interwoven branches right beside the path in a little clearing. The door stood open and he bent to look inside. His gaze fell on a golden crown placed on a throne. His immediate thought was to take it for himself, so he leaned further and encircled the crown with his arm. Delighted with his prize, he cantered down the track but in an instant his elation turned to terrible apprehension as he heard an iron voice shout: 'Put down that crown you have stolen! Defend yourself!'

He turned in terror; moments later he was struck by a spear and fell from his horse, where he lay on the path unable to move or to speak.

There he lay for hours and would have died had Galahad not found him.

'What has happened? Who has wounded you?' he cried, sliding off his horse and kneeling beside the youth.

He took him in his arms and tried to raise him. Then he, too, heard a horse galloping towards him. It was the man who had wounded Melias.

'Look to yourself!' he shouted, and rode straight at Galahad with his spear. He missed his aim and Galahad, on foot though he was, swung his sword in a great furious stroke and cut off the man's arm at the elbow. At this, he screamed and fled.

With great difficulty Galahad got Melias to a Benedictine abbey, where the brother infirmarian volunteered to take care of him and declared that Melias would recover, given proper care and rest.

Melias begged Galahad to stay with him, but he hardened himself against the youth's plea, having already delayed several days to make sure of his recovery.

'I must follow up the quest' he said, 'now I know that you are safe.'

Melias was still unhappy and tried every means he could think of to secure Galahad's presence, but the brother encouraged Galahad to continue his journey.

'This young man would not be here but for his arrogance and greed' he said.

Then Melias made many promises to follow Galahad once he had recovered.

'I will catch up with you' he said, 'and we can seek the Grail together.'

Galahad said goodbye to him; and in all the years of his quest he never caught sight of Melias again, nor heard any word of him.

Meanwhile, as luck would have it, Gawain and Hector found themselves asking for shelter at the very abbey where the famous shield had been housed. Soon they heard that the shield had gone, given to Galahad who had been the monks' guest a week ago.

'What is this shield?' asked Hector.

'It is a white shield with a red cross' they told him. 'It belonged to the son of Joseph of Arimathea but now it belongs to Galahad. Look out for it on your travels. You will surely meet up with him.'

They lost no time but they found no trace of Galahad or his shield. They rode over heathland where they met occasional shepherds watching over great flocks of sheep. Presently the heath-land became a sombre beech forest, with few or no flowers growing in the shade beneath the heavy crowns of the trees.

A Kind of Travelling

This was the part of the forest through which Galahad and Melias had ridden; and when Gawain and Hector were clear of it, they came to a good, newly-made road which led to the Benedictine monastery where Melias was recovering from his wound.

They found him in bed in the infirmary where an aged monk was reading to him from the adventures of St. Brendan.

'Is Galahad here?' Gawain asked him.

But he got the same answer as before: 'He left here some days ago.'

'We have lost him twice' said Gawain savagely. He was in no mood to listen to Melias' story of how Galahad got the shield, and how Galahad had rescued him in the forest.

'We mustn't waste time here' he told the youth. 'No doubt I shall catch up with Galahad before long. At least I shall recognise his shield and then we may have more luck on this quest. Tell me, which direction did he go?'

No one replied, but the old monk who had been reading to Melias said under his breath:

'You are not likely to find him.'

Gawain heard him.

'Why not?' he said sharply.

The monk said 'You are not the man to ride with him.'

Gawain was incensed by this and, had the brother not been a monk he would have paid for these words.

'You know nothing about me' said Gawain contemptuously. 'Why should I not be his companion?'

The brother said softly 'Sir, one day you will hear why', and he took his book and went away.

Next day the two knights went to hear Mass in the abbey church. They stood at the back with other guests and a few women from the nearby village. A heavy stone grille painted in gold and blue cut them off from the monks.

The Mass began. The knights and the village people could see little or nothing of the altar. This did not worry them; they were used to having no part in the ritual. The priest said the prayers and made the offerings mostly in silence. Even had he spoken aloud no one would have heard him because a great group of monks and novices sang with great vigour. Seeing and hearing nothing, the two knights turned their attention to the coloured glass windows, but these were too high to yield much interest. Failing that, they studied the painting on the wall beside them. It was painted in yellows, reds and blacks on the grey stone, and showed a huge scaly fish standing upright, its jaws wide open. Into this mouth of hell the souls of men and women were being flung by angels armed with spears and pitchforks. One angel stood apart with a great black key in his hand; evidently his role was to lock up the fish's mouth so that no one could escape.

Hector and Gawain soon turned away from this dispiriting scene and set themselves to saying the prayers they knew by heart: the Lord's Prayer and the

Hail Mary. Before long, the choir fell silent, the church emptied, and the two knights rode off towards a landscape of rolling hills.

★

While Gawain and Hector were leaving the abbey, Galahad was riding steadily towards a great grassy mound which held the ruin of some old building. He sat there for a time and asked God what he should do next; for, like Gawain and Hector, he had no clear idea of where he ought to go. Then a voice came to him, directing him to a castle which he could see away to the west, standing beside a broad river. The voice said: 'That is the Castle of the Maidens, a place of pain and injustice. Go there and set the prisoners free.'

Without hesitation Galahad set off. In the streets and from the market-stalls that were built against the castle walls, men and women pressed forward to see him. He could hardly pass them, so great was the crowd, so intense their scrutiny. Then a group of women urged him to turn back. Hardly had they spoken when a squire rode out from the castle gates, asking Galahad what he wanted. He said plainly: 'I am here to free the prisoners.'

The squire returned, and presently a group of seven mounted men emerged who rode at Galahad with furious shouts, their lances at the ready, shields hung round their necks, swords at their left hips.

Galahad stood firm and Mordrain's old shield protected him against all their onslaughts. Defying the knights, he charged storming, shouting, thrusting with his lance. He pressed them hard and drove them on until their courage failed, they lost cohesion and fled each one of them before him.

Galahad did not go after them. Instead he waited for the castle gates to be opened. Then he rode into the courtyard while the onlookers shouted and cheered, and cried out:

'Blessed be God who led you here!'

'Long life to the knight with the red cross!'

'Stay with us, sir, and protect us!'

The priest rang the bells in the church, the lady of the castle came to greet him, and the whole fortress was suddenly full of celebration and singing. For Galahad had rescued not only the lady of the castle but also the many other women whom the seven knights had imprisoned there. By stealth these men had seized the castle, had declared war on all the neighbouring lords and made themselves the evil rulers of the whole countryside.

Rumours about the Castle of the Maidens had spread far and wide; tales of the fiery stars that had fallen onto it from heaven; of stones in its walls that had bled tears of blood at the sight of such injustice and cruelty.

When Galahad heard all this he began to invite all the local lords to the castle and he gradually prevailed on them, one by one, to give their loyalty to its lady.

When they saw how capable he was and how men listened to him despite his youth, the townspeople and the knights of the castle begged Galahad to stay;

but after some days he took his leave of them. As he was riding out they brought him news, saying: 'Sir, those seven knights you defeated, who ran from you, they have all been killed and their bodies are scattered all over the hillside.'

'Who could have killed them?' he asked, surprised. 'They were wounded and exhausted men. No knight would kill men in such a state.'

'It was Gawain and Hector who did it' they told him. 'Knights like yourself on the quest of the Grail. Men saw them do it. They recognised Gawain by the black hawk on his shield.'

Then Galahad rode away, wondering how such a thing could happen.

★

Leaving the seven knights dead, Hector and Gawain argued as to which road to take.

Hector said 'We'll find nothing in the direction we came from, nor in the area you've travelled. Let's look for a new road.'

They rode together past the hill, away from the river, until they entered a stretch of lonely forest where they met neither men nor beasts, and where even the birds were silent.

They rode all day, and at dusk they chanced on the ruins of a chapel. Its thatched roof had been burned and the beams were blackened. All round were signs of devastation and the ashes of old fires. Small saplings of aspen had begun to repopulate the earth where fire had charred it.

They looked around this cheerless place which offered little or no shelter for the night, and then settled themselves in the roofless chapel against one of the walls.

It grew dark, a misty night without stars or moonlight, and such sleep as they had was full of dreams and apprehensions.

Hector awoke suddenly and roused Gawain.

'I am concerned for my brother Lancelot' he said, 'for I have seen him in a dream. I saw him captured and led away until he came to a spring where he wanted to drink the water. But whenever he leaned down to drink, the water sank deeper so that he could never quench his thirst. And I saw my own self in the dream, too. I was riding to a celebration in a king's house and when I got to the door, they opened it and turned me away and said "There is no place here for you."

'What can this mean?' he cried. 'What will happen to Lancelot and me on this quest? I shall never rest until I hear some news of him.'

As they sat pondering and fearful they saw a light approaching them. As it came into the chapel it showed itself as a lighted candle held in a man's hand, with a horse's bridle hanging from the wrist.

The vision paused in front of them and then it vanished. In the darkness a voice spoke to them from the ruined chapel:

'Weak men!' it said, 'Blind and violent men! Learn from the hand, the candle and the bridle, or your quest will come to nothing.'

They were amazed.

'Did you hear those words?' asked Hector.

'I did' said Gawain in consternation. 'Let us get away from here and find someone to tell us what they mean.'

As soon as it was dawn they saddled the horses and set off in haste, riding down into a valley where they asked a man carrying a load of wood if there was some hermit or recluse nearby.

He indicated a narrow track that led towards a wooded hill a good deal further on.

They rode in silence, and Gawain grew steadily more incensed because this quest was offering nothing he had expected.

All at once he heard a shout as an unknown knight rode towards them from the trees. He was fully armed, his lance ready, his face guarded.

At the sight of him all thought of hermits fled from Gawain's mind. His face set hard in anger.

'That man is threatening us' he shouted.

In an instant and with no thought of the consequences, he hooked the chain-mail guard across his face and spurred his horse towards the stranger. The force of the encounter unhorsed them both but while Gawain struggled to his feet, the other man lay prostrate, transfixed by Gawain's lance which had snapped. Gawain took out his sword and went to kill the fallen man but he begged for mercy.

Gawain stood over him. 'Who are you?' he said.

He answered 'I am Owen of Eskdale in Cumbria. I am one of King Arthur's men and I have been on this quest a long time.'

At this news Gawain was filled with fury that fate had led him to attack a brother knight. He hoped that Owen would not recognise him but the dying man said:

'I know you, Gawain. No one is more brave than you. You inspired us to go on this quest. Help me pull out this lance and get me to some abbey, for I feel that my time is short.'

They did not know what to do.

'Help me to lift him up' said Hector. 'I will hold him.'

Owen cried out in torment with the spear shaft embedded in his chest. Gawain took hold of the shaft and wrenched it out. Owen was convulsed in agony, and he died almost immediately.

Now they had to search for some church abbey in which to bury him. They found a small church dedicated to St. Martin, built beside a churchyard. Here they buried him on the south side. The cemetery had no gravestones because the local people used it for assemblies and markets, and celebrating saints' days. So Gawain left money for a stone to be put in the church which was to read:

NEARBY IS THE BODY OF SIR OWEN OF ESKDALE IN CUMBRIA, WHOM GAWAIN SLEW IN COMBAT WHEN BOTH WERE SEARCHING FOR THE GRAIL.'

When this was done, they resumed their journey in deep gloom and disappointment, taking the path suggested by the parish priest.
'The hermit who lives in that cave is known far and wide' he said. 'He will certainly be able to help you, none better. He has cures for every ailment.'
The track led them up a hill so steep that they had to leave the horses and go on foot. Towards the top of the hill, the rough grass gave way to rocks, and there they found an old man about to enter a cave. He held a wicker basket containing many sorts of plants, and he looked sharply at his visitors.
When the two had regained their breath they asked the old man for help, and followed him into his home which turned out to be two caves. It was hot in the inner cave because the hermit was boiling crushed leaves and wild garlic with pig's fat, to make an ointment for sprains and stiffness.
'Are you sick or wounded?' he asked. 'I have many herbs to heal you, though it depends on the will of God and the state of the moon. When the moon is waning no one will do well.'
They said they wanted help of a different kind, and told him about the vision in the chapel, and about the fatal encounter with Owen.
The hermit listened without interruption. Then he spoke.
'I doubt if I can help you' he said. 'You seem to me to be misguided men who should have stayed at home. Tell me again about that vision in the chapel.'
They repeated the story. Then he said:
'Take your mind from the shell of the nut to its kernel. In other words, consider the meaning of what you saw. That lighted candle stands for God's action in this world. The hand holding it stands for human compassion, and the bridle round the man's wrist stands for restraint. You both lack restraint, you both lack compassion. You do nothing to show God's presence in the world. And the knight you killed last week' he told them, 'is not the only one. You also killed the seven knights who fought with Galahad, even though they asked you for mercy. You are no more than assassins and murderers.'
They were taken aback at this, wondering how he knew, for they had not thought to mention the seven knights.
He went on. 'Galahad fought these knights but he would never kill wounded, beaten men. He let them go, and you destroyed them. One thing is certain. You must make amends; you must do penance for that killing.'
'What sort of penance?' they cried.
'Whatever I shall decide is suitable.'
Gawain tried to justify himself.
'Sir, our whole life on this quest is penance' he said. 'We have met one hardship after another. We have had nothing but bad luck.'

The Rowan Tree

'Look at the tree beside my door' said the hermit.

They both turned to stare at the grey bark, the red berries, the dark green leaves.

'This is the lovely rowan tree' said the hermit. 'It is God's blessed tree. It guards us against evil; it calms human anger and violence.'

He broke off a twig and offered it to Gawain.

'Take this with you' he said. 'You could both be like this rowan, full of life and greenness; but you are more like dried up withered trees, seeking only power and reputation. You have both forgotten what Nescien told you, that this is a journey into God's mysteries.'

Gawain did not take the twig. He looked away, his face hard.

'I thank you for your words' he said, 'and I will think about them when my quest is over.'

The hermit said: 'Remember what you both promised when you became knights: Never to use your sword, or any sword, to injure anyone unjustly. Your work is to protect the Church, avenge the wrongs of the poor, and keep the country in a state of peace. How much of that have you done on your quest?'

They listened in angry silence and Gawain said in his heart 'We are wasting our time here.'

Finally, the hermit stood up, implying that their meeting was over.

'Did you think' he said, 'that the quest would bring you prizes, or money or fame? It will give you none of these.'

They retraced their steps dejected and sullen, hardly speaking to each other. Their hearts were no longer on their journey and they rode aimlessly across the land. They stayed in monasteries, in pilgrims' hostels or with foresters, and they kept well away from hermitages.

When it was almost winter they heard about a tournament planned to take place before a castle a few miles further on. This raised their spirits somewhat, because with luck and skill they might each win prizes and ransoms. For the rule was that each knight who surrendered had to forfeit his armour and his horse to his conqueror. Gawain had fought in many tournaments, and in single combat jousts as well, not only with lances and swords, but with axes too, and he had no fear of any opponent. Had he not been Arthur's nephew, he might well have become one of the roving knights who spent their whole lives going from one tournament to another for the sake of the rewards.

They rode on swiftly to the castle and found the tournament at its height. It had developed into a dangerous and fierce battle between the knights of the castle – all of them in green surcoats and with green banners – and a group of roving freelance knights intent on plunder; men drawn from far and near. All were armed with lances and swords, some with axes or maces, while a few even carried long iron poles with hooks, useful tools for dragging men off their horses.

Gawain and Hector joined with this group, and before long the ferocity and skill they brought turned the tournament into something of a rout. The green knights fell back, their cohesion broken.

Then suddenly a new wave of strength seemed to flow into them, and Gawain saw the shield he had heard of. It was Galahad's white shield with its rough red cross. Galahad was grimly fighting off these attackers, dealing heavy blows from the saddle. Then he flung forward to Gawain, whom he did not recognise. They met in a great collision which cracked both their shields. Their long ash lances were too strong to snap; they only bent under the impact.

Again they charged and this time Gawain's shield gave way. He lost his stirrups, was flung hard against the cantle of his saddle, and fell beside his horse which did not flinch, but stood motionless beside him as it had been trained to do.

Without hesitation Hector rode to Gawain's rescue and stood beside him, defending him. In the furious melee Galahad rode past him, and was lost to Hector's sight.

When the herald finally brought the tournament to an end, Hector helped to carry the unconscious Gawain into the castle. He was badly wounded and lay senseless for days. Hector feared he would die but the castle had a herbalist who reassured him, saying:

'You will see that when the moon begins to wax he will grow better.'

Meanwhile he treated Gawain with great care, and covered his pillow with herbs to bring back his senses.

Weeks later, when he was himself again though marked badly by his wound, Gawain thought of the sword and the stone that had floated in the river beside Camelot.

'Do you remember' he said to Hector, 'how I tried to pull it out and Lancelot warned me? He said that whoever tried to take it out would be cut down by that sword. Well, that has been my lot. I have been cut by it, and now I am giving up this quest. For me it has led to nothing.'

Gawain remained in the castle until after Christmas, slowly regaining his strength. Then he said goodbye to Hector and rode back to Arthur's court.

The castle was dark and nearly deserted, though there were servants and dependants enough, and the usual groups of beggars and wanderers sheltering in the castle depths.

He found the king wrapped in a thick cloak against the cold, sitting by a window watching the falling snow. It was a gloomy welcome for Gawain.

Arthur embraced his nephew but his heart was with the knights still on their journey. Fear and apprehension fell on him as he foresaw the possible consequences of this quest: his castle abandoned; his thirty kingdoms, the admiration of the world, broken; his band of knights, dearer to him than Guinevere ever was, divided, scattered and destroyed.

'I am in great sorrow' he told Gawain. 'So many of these men will not return.'

Tears ran down his face.

'I fear that I shall lose you all. This is my greatest grief.'

CHAPTER 3

Towards the Sea

Just as Gawain and Hector met by chance, so Lancelot and Parcival meet and ride together, though after a disagreement Lancelot goes on alone. Parcival pauses to take stock, to ask advice from a woman recluse who tells him something about the mysterious Grail castle, and about the outcome of the quest itself. Delighted by this knowledge and blind to danger, he falls victim to evil spirits and the hostile forces of nature. He is only rescued when he obeys a voice from the other world commanding him to take a boat, leave everything behind and trust himself to the unknown sea.

Parcival rode alone through the forest for weeks on end, stopping at pilgrims' hostels as he went. He found himself following a river, and one day he came to a fishing-station where men caught salmon in the falls. As he stood marvelling at the coracles the fishermen used on the river, for he had never seen such boats, he was surprised and happy to find Lancelot, whom chance had brought to this same spot. They spent that night lodging with the parish priest, and next day they agreed to ride together.

They were an ill-assorted pair. Lancelot was known everywhere as Arthur's right hand, respected and acclaimed for his courage and fortitude, while Parcival was only a young knight lacking any fame at all.

Lancelot was glad of his company. He knew the story of Parcival's family, of Pellinore and Ashfleur, his parents. Pellinore had become one of Arthur's knights and on his death in battle, Ashfleur had fled for safety into the depths of Wales with a few servants and friends and her last remaining child. Here amid lakes and forests Parcival had grown up, deliberately kept away from the world of violence by his mother's efforts. But one day the boy had met a posse of knights and the encounter determined him to find King Arthur and to claim knighthood for himself.

As they rode along Lancelot remembered how Arthur had said of Parcival 'This little Welsh man may well make a true knight, though I doubt if he'll live to see the day.' For Parcival, knight though he was now, remained unpredictable and reckless, too.

One day they arrived at a busy village with a fast-flowing stream and a water-mill. The priest's house was near the pond, in front of the stone church. A path cut through the village, with thatched cabins and barns on either side. Somewhat set apart was a thatched wooden house, and here the two knights

23

paused, for a voice called to them from the open window: 'God be with you both!' and a woman leaned from the window.

'Who can she be?' Parcival asked, and Lancelot told him; 'She is a recluse, a woman who never leaves the house. She spends her time in prayer, and people go to her for counsel.'

They returned her greeting, and were about to ride on when a strange knight appeared from behind the church walls and rode swiftly towards them.

'This is no knight of King Arthur's!' cried Parcival. 'Look at his shield!'

Neither of them had seen Galahad's red and white shield before; moreover, his helmet let them see only the upper part of his face. Believing that he was an enemy, Lancelot and Parcival rode towards him, Lancelot charging with his lance. In return, Galahad returned the blow so fiercely that he swept the older man backwards off his horse; and then without hesitation he turned on Parcival with his sword. He struck him such a blow that the metal of his helmet was dented. Parcival slid off his horse, the sound ringing in his ears, his eyes bedazzled with stars, and lay there in the dust not knowing whether he was alive or dead. Dimly he heard the voice of the recluse, but who she spoke to he could not make out, nor what she said.

By the time the two had recovered their wits Galahad had ridden far away out of the village, across the heathland and into an oak forest. Both men, Lancelot in particular, were furiously angry at their humiliation at the hands of this stranger, and they set off together in pursuit. They did not find their quarry, and presently Parcival grew tired of the fruitless search. He hung back and remonstrated, but Lancelot was not to be deflected, so they parted company.

In the evening Parcival retraced his steps to the home of the recluse, where he found the window closed. He was undeterred and rapped on the wooden shutter in a peremptory manner. There was no reply, so he knocked again and called loudly. At this, the woman opened the window again and said to him:

'God guard you, sir. What is your name?'

'I am Parcival, the Welsh knight' he said.

At this she called for a servant to admit him. Another servant took his horse and then showed him to a small room where a fire was burning.

'You may sleep here' he told him. 'The recluse will see you in the morning.'

Next day she summoned Parcival and asked how she might help him.

'I think you knew that knight with the white shield' he said, 'the one that passed this way yesterday. It seemed to me that you spoke to him.'

'Why do you wish to know?'

'You can judge for yourself' he said. 'You saw how that man beat us, humbled us, yet Lancelot is the greatest of King Arthur's knights.'

'So you seek revenge?' she said. 'Are you as reckless as your father and your brothers, who were all killed one after the other?'

Parcival was silenced by this, for it seemed that the recluse must know something about his family. In answer to his question she said:

'I do know you well, though we have never met before. Your mother Ashfleur was my sister. I knew that she fled to the Snow Mountains for safety. When did you last see her?'

He was abashed and said 'Never since I left her. I have often dreamed of going back. I have tried to go back but I could never find the way.'

'Your mother is dead' said his aunt. 'She died of grief because you left her.'

They were silent for a time, and Parcival crossed himself. He remembered his mother telling him that this was one of the best Christian prayers and would keep evil at bay.

His aunt said 'You may wonder why I live as a recluse when once I was a queen. My husband died in the wars and then I came here to live beside this church of our Lady. I brought a few servants for protection, and a chaplain. Now I have set myself to pray and to listen to the scriptures, so that I may make a good end to my life.'

Parcival remained with her for two days, and during this time she told him that the knight who had defeated him and Lancelot was Galahad.

'He is the son of Lancelot and Elaine' she said. 'His mother was the daughter of King Pelles who lives in Carbonek, the castle where the Grail is. That shield you did not recognise was given to him by the White monks, and he is its rightful owner.'

Parcival was taken aback by these words and wondered how she knew so much. As though she could read his thoughts, she said:

'Parcival, you must never dream of harming Galahad. He is the knight Merlin spoke of when he kept a seat for him at the Round Table. What is more, Merlin knew that Galahad would find the Grail.'

'Then' said Parcival, 'the only thing I wish is to find him and to ride with him.'

He thought suddenly of Ashfleur in Snowdonia, and said: 'My mother used to give me good advice. She told me to be sure to travel with good men. "Never go with any man" she said, "unless you know who he is." Now I will have the best companion anyone could have. Do you know where Galahad may have gone?'

She was hesitant. At last she said: 'No, but surely he is making his way to Castle Carbonek.'

He asked where Carbonek might lie, but she knew no more than he did.

'I have only heard about it. They say it is built in a place where no storms ever come; where the sun and moon and stars all shine together and can be seen even in daylight. But others say it stands on some rocky headland on the coast of Wales, or even at the very edge of the world. They say that only God knows where it is because it is always hidden in mists so that no human efforts can find it. Be that as it may, I believe that you will meet Galahad before too long. When you have done so, events will indicate your path.'

When he heard this, Parcival was anxious to get on his way, and he rode off happily, all his heart set on finding Galahad. He made his way down a green lane into a forest full of birds. Between the green leaves he could see the sunlight pouring down, giving itself in energy and life to everything that grew. It was high summer and he could hear the sound of a church bell. He turned towards it and before long he reached a Cistercian abbey. This, though he did not know it, was the very place where Galahad had received his shield.

The monks welcomed him and gave him a place to sleep. At dawn next day Parcival went into the cold church. Like the abbey, it was totally without decoration or carved pillars or silver shrines for relics. Across the narrow nave, an iron screen cut off the celebrating priest from any layfolk who might present themselves.

Parcival stood near the screen, seeing nothing of the priest's actions, hearing nothing of the silent prayers that accompanied them. The church was not only cold, but dark as well, with only a single candle to illuminate it. Soon he was well into his own private prayers, mostly repetitions of the 'Hail Mary' as taught by Ashfleur in Snowdonia, when he fancied he saw a flicker of gold beside the altar. He peered through the interstices of the screen and thought he saw a recumbent figure covered with a golden cloth. He stared hard and made out the figure of an old, old man. When the Mass was over, the priest went to a pillar on which a gilt container was affixed. He took something from the container and went to the old man. Parcival wondered what he was doing.

He asked one of the monks to explain what he had just seen.

'The old man you saw is King Mordrain' the monk told him. 'He was the friend of Joseph of Arimathea and his sons. He came here to die years ago but he has lived on ever since. He says he is waiting till Joseph's last descendant will come to say goodbye to him.'

'How old is he?' asked Parcival in awe.

'He must be four hundred years or more.'

When he had digested this, Parcival asked the monk: 'What did the priest take to him?'

'It was the Eucharistic bread.'

At this Parcival marvelled. 'I have never seen it myself' he said. 'I have never seen it given to anyone.'

The monk said disapprovingly 'No lay man ought to see the host, for no one is worthy. And many priests who do see it are not worthy either. It is true that in some places nowadays they begin to show it to the people, but I don't agree with it. God preserve us from new things! In the old days people were forbidden even to look at it.'

Parcival said goodbye and rode away between fields of barley. He was pleased with everything he saw, and his mind was full of the thought of meeting Galahad. His way soon led into a forest where the monks were making a clearing, dragging the felled trees away with oxen. He rode on, his mind still on Galahad, quite forgetful of danger.

Towards the Sea

Then he heard the approach of horses, as a troop of twenty armed men emerged from a side track and barred his way. Their surcoats and shields were black, and one of them carried a black pennant with the yellow device of a dragon.

'Who are you?' they shouted. 'Where do you come from?'

He was completely taken by surprise.

'From the court of King Arthur' he said.

At that, they shouted:

'Destroy him! Don't let him live! Cut him down!'

And the whole troop came at him with a great roar.

The skill of Lancelot might have beaten off the men but Parcival was by no means such a warrior. He defended himself, he fought grimly, sending one knight to the ground, ramming his lance into a second horse and felling horse and rider together. When his own lance was torn away, he dealt blows with his two-edged sword but he could not beat off so many men. He was dragged off his horse and fell to the ground. He struggled to one knee and took his sword again. He knew he had no hope of surviving. At that moment, above all the shouting he heard a great voice calling, and he knew that it was Galahad's.

Immediately, the pattern of the attack changed. Galahad thundered in behind him and cut a clean path through the attackers, slashing with his sword held in both hands; while his horse never swerved, being well used to battle. Galahad drove the rest of the knights before him, and he and they vanished deep into the trees, leaving Parcival bruised and beaten on the forest floor.

He scrambled up and shouted to Galahad: 'Wait for me!' but he had no chance to catch up with his rescuer, for he had no horse. Without a horse, a knight was nothing. Yet he went on foot, awkwardly enough and full of frustration.

He stumped along the woodland path, growing ever more exhausted, and hampered by his shield and sword. The day faded, and finally he fell down against an ancient oak tree. Tears of mortification rolled down his crimson weary face. At length, he fell asleep.

When he awoke, the wind had strengthened and all the branches overhead were swaying. He looked around at the dark shadowy places, and in the thin light of the moon he saw a woman standing in front of him. He thought she was a phantom but she spoke to him.

'What are you doing in this forest?' she asked

'I am doing nothing' he answered angrily, 'but if I had a horse, I would be doing something. I would be searching for my friend.'

'I can get a horse for you' she said, 'the best horse you ever rode, and I promise that it will take you wherever you want to go.'

At these words, his spirits rose. He looked expectantly at the woman, never dreaming that he was being deceived.

'Wait for me' she told him, and presently she came back leading the horse.

A sort of dread came over Parcival when he saw this horse in the moonlight, for it was taller and more massive than any he had ever ridden, black with thick coarse hair, a short wiry mane that stood erect, and a wild eye. It halted before him and, when he hauled himself into the saddle not without difficulty, the beast still remained motionless until the woman spoke to it. Then the horse moved off through the clearing. Without warning its gait changed, and soon Parcival found that he had no control over it.

The horse galloped through the wood into open country and this furious ride seemed to him to go on for days. The horse took him through a valley towards a wide and fiercely flowing river, and when they came to the river's edge Parcival was convinced that he would drown. He thought of his mother's advice and hastily called on God for help, making the sign of a cross on his helmet. At this the horse uttered a neighing scream, flinging Parcival to the ground. Then it plunged into the moonlit water, and he saw sheets of fire rise from the dark surface and turn the horse to ashes.

He lay bruised and horribly shocked, and it was a long time before he came to himself. When he opened his eyes this time, he saw no river, no trees. He saw only the grey endless sea. He found that he was lying on a grassy island with rocky outcrops at its highest point. Seabirds flew overhead and wild creatures roamed over the stones.

He was not only bewildered but very much afraid, and thought he might be safer if he climbed the rocks. As he was doing so, he heard screams and he saw a winged serpent dragging away a small lion cub, while an adult lion roared in fury.

'The cub is calling for help' thought Parcival, and he turned back drawing his sword. The serpent breathed out blasts so hot that his shield could barely protect him, but he struck hard and severed the beast's head so that the cub fell uninjured. The lion now ran to Parcival, who feared it might attack him, but instead it rubbed itself against him with every sign of gratitude and friendship. That night it stayed beside him, having taken the cub away to its den. So Parcival and the lion became companions, spending their days together and their nights side by side among the rocks.

Parcival examined the island, which had never a tree but only sand, shingle and rocks. He could see no other land, only the cold sea which seemed to stretch to the world's edge. By the third day he thought he would starve to death, but as he lay listlessly watching the waves break on the little circular bay, his attention was caught by a white sail. As fast as he could, he made his way down to the bay, leaving his helmet and sword behind.

The ship came to rest as though it were anchored.

'Thank God you have come!' Parcival cried to the old man who stood on board. 'I thought I would never get away from this place. I am in great danger. I must get back to land.'

'Where are you from?' asked the old man, who was dressed like a priest in white vestments.

'From King Arthur's court' Parcival said. 'I am one of the knights searching for the Grail. But how I ever got on to this island, only God knows!'

Then he asked in his turn: 'Sir, where have you come from? How did you find me?'

'I have come from the other world' he said, 'to warn you to expect more dangers on your quest.'

'I shall never finish that quest unless I get away from here' said Parcival in an impatient voice.

'You may still do so' the priest said, 'but be warned by me: Don't believe everyone you meet. You have already been deceived by the woman and her black horse. She was a devil who took human shape, but you were too simple to see it. Well, you will meet others like her.'

With these words the ship sailed away with him and left the downcast Parcival still marooned.

On the fourth day he was so weak with hunger that he lay down miserably beside the lion which watched over him. At midday, as he was staring over the sea, he thought he saw a disturbance in the water, a pillar of foam turning and spinning. It came towards the island at a great speed and revealed itself as a ship of quite another kind. Its sails and rigging were black, its timbers were tarred black and it flew a white and purple pennant.

With great efforts he got himself to the water's edge. This vessel, like the white ship before it, came to rest so close that Parcival could see the woman who leaned from it to speak to him. 'Poor man!' she called. 'Has no one tried to take you from this terrible place?'

'No one' he cried, and he noticed that she was dressed in purple and crimson, and was more beautiful than any woman he had ever seen before. 'No one' he said again. 'Will you take me with you?'

'That is why I have come' she said. 'I know who you are. I know that you are a friend of Galahad's and want to find him. Rest assured, I saw him a day or two ago chasing two hostile knights across a river. I can take you to him.'

At this news, Parcival's spirits soared.

'Shall I take you to him, Parcival?' she asked. He was surprised that she knew his name and, in turn, he asked her who she was.

'My name does not matter' she said. 'All you need know is that I am the victim of terrible injustice and that you can help me. I once stood highest of all at the court of a great king; and then without warning he cast me down and expelled me. He left me with nothing, and so now I go around the world looking for men who will become my knights and avenge me.'

Two sailors from the ship now set up a splendid tent on the white sand, and she and Parcival sat in its shade on straw-filled cushions. He could hardly restrain himself when he saw tables being set up and food arriving. He was famished for he had eaten nothing for four days. Roasted goose, venison steaks, mutton stewed with cinnamon and saffron, dates cooked in wine, he tackled them all as though they might vanish out of his reach.

A Kind of Travelling

The lady went on recounting her misfortunes while he ate; and though he was sympathetic, he only half listened to her. Then the sailors brought out jug after jug of wine. This wine was a far cry from his mother's blackberry cordial in Snowdonia, and he drank so avidly that he began to get confused and to see the lady from the ship as the most wonderful woman he had ever known, and the most unjustly treated, and the most desirable.

He made reckless promises of the help he would give her in her fight for justice, and it was not long before they were both in bed together in the tent.

Suddenly, Parcival saw his sword standing upright, resting against his armour. The moon shone clearly on the enamel cross on its hilt. Instantly, he thought of the woman in the forest, the black horse, the warnings of the old man. He leapt up and made a great sign of the cross over himself.

At that very moment, the wind rose to a great scream, the tent and bed tore themselves loose and dissolved into ashes that rained down from the sky. A vast sea enveloped the ship. As for the lady, he saw her drawn up into the sky.

'You have betrayed me!' she shrieked as she turned in the wind, and he lost sight of her.

Now Parcival was truly terrified. He was also full of fury at his own blindness. He threw himself down on the sand and lay there. It was hours later when he heard a voice. The priest in the white ship had come back. He stood beside Parcival, looking down on him, asking 'How have things gone since I left you?'

'Everything went wrong' said Parcival, and told him the whole story.

'Do you know who the lady in the black ship is?' the priest asked.

'No, but I suppose the fiend must have sent her.'

'She was the arch fiend himself, Lucifer, whom God cast down from heaven. Oh man, you don't learn quickly, you believe everything you hear. You may have a good heart, but you have no judgement whatsoever.'

'Let me sail with you' Parcival begged, but the priest refused.

'I have many other people who need help from me' he said. 'I cannot stay with you, but I will leave the ship with you.'

At this he went back to the world he had come from, leaving Parcival staring unhappily at the empty ship. He had no wish to have it; he had never set foot in a ship in his whole life. Presently, he heard a commanding voice which said to him:

'Parcival, take your armour and get aboard that ship as I direct you. Let it take you as the seas decide. You must leave everything behind you now.'

Parcival was in deadly fear of the sea and had never sailed on it. He hesitated, full of doubts, but he dared not disobey. At last he put on his armour, took his sword and battered shield, and went carefully on board through the shallow water. A breeze sprang up that rippled the surface of the sea. He could feel the light wind on his face. Then the ship took him far away.

CHAPTER 4

The Nine Stars in the Sky

Once he has left Parcival, Lancelot finds that all his skill and good fortune have deserted him. Troubled and bewildered, he breaks off his journey to lodge with a hermit, hoping to be offered a solution to his problem. After much debate the hermit prevails on Lancelot to admit that his heart is divided, set on Queen Guinevere rather than on the quest. Herein lies his problem. In great despondency Lancelot rides away. Only later does he get new heart when he sees a majestic apparition in the night sky.

Once Parcival had parted company from him, Lancelot rode on determined to find the knight who had felled him; but no matter how far he rode he caught no glimpse of Galahad. Yet he would not give up and pressed on until darkness fell.

Now only the light of the moon filtered through the oak leaves. Presently he found himself at a crossroads in the forest, and nearby in the clearing he saw a tiny chapel. Beside the chapel, which seemed half ruined and deserted, stood a stone cross taller than he was. The surface of the stone was decorated with strange spirals and interlacings of which he could make nothing.

'This must have been made by people in the old days' he thought.

He looked hard at the chapel and it seemed to him that some extra radiance lighted up the windows. He went to investigate, and found to his surprise that the interior was aglow with candlelight. He could see a silver altar covered with white linen cloths, and on it a six-branched lighted candlestick also made of silver.

The windows were heavily barred but the door was open. He made to go inside but some invisible force resisted him. He was puzzled and dismayed by this strange happening; but realising that he could not spend the night in the chapel, he hobbled his horse, removed his helmet, sword and shield, and set himself to sleep at the base of the standing stone.

When he awoke around midnight, unsure whether he was awake or half sleeping, he heard the approach of horses and the sound of a man's voice. Two figures came towards him, one a squire leading a horse, the other a sick man lying on the horse litter. The man's voice was raised in prayer and he kept saying 'Oh God, heal me. Oh God, cure my sickness.'

The squire laid the sick man between the chapel door and the stone cross, and Lancelot saw how both of them turned to look at him lying there. He looked back but found he had no power to say a word to them.

From then onwards everything took on the quality of a nightmare. Lancelot could neither move nor respond but lay in a dull, heavy torpor. He saw the silver altar move out of the chapel and come to rest beside the praying knight. Even more, he saw the hidden Grail come down onto the altar; the very Grail he had seen in Camelot and had sworn to search for. But now nothing had any meaning for him, not even the cries and thankgiving of the sick man now healed by the Grail. Nothing touched his heart; he might have been a stone effigy lying on a tomb.

After what seemed many hours, the Grail and the altar vanished. The knight and his squire went over to where Lancelot lay.

'Who can this man be?' said the squire, looking hard at him. 'To lie there and ignore the Grail, he must be under some spell.'

His master said 'He must have something on his conscience.'

They both studied Lancelot's shield but neither was familiar with its wavy bands of blue and white.

'Could he be one of those knights who are searching for the Grail?' said the squire, but the knight gave a great laugh.

"Does he look like a man searching for something?'

Then, since the sick man had brought neither horse nor arms with him, they commandeered Lancelot's helmet, shield and sword, unhobbled his horse and rode away with it.

When dawn broke, Lancelot was himself again, fully awake and alert.

'Last night must have been a dream' he told himself. He went once more to the chapel where the door was open, but he was still unable to set foot in it. His efforts met the same resistance as before. He could see that the chapel was empty.

He stood staring into it quite bewildered when he heard a voice calling him. It seemed as though the whole forest was calling him to account.

'Lancelot, Lancelot!' it cried, 'Take yourself away from this chapel. You have no right to be here. They call you leader of the knights, but you are a man harder than stone, more bitter than bark. You are more fruitless than the fig-tree.'

He was filled with consternation. He looked round the clearing, hurried to get his armour and his horse. All were gone. In that moment he knew that it had not been a dream, and he gave vent to terrible grief and disappointment.

'What has happened to me?' he cried. 'What has gone wrong? I am searching for the Grail and I see it and do nothing. I fight some unknown knight and he strikes me down. I try to enter the chapel and it forbids me. My horse and my armour have been stolen.'

Realising his plight, he cried again: 'My God, what is happening to me? Even my sword has been taken. That sword has never failed me in the past; all my own strength flowed into that blade. Now I have no sword, and all my power is gone.'

He was filled with half-spoken dread and self-reproach, and thought:

'Has this come on me because I am not single-hearted in my search, because I am divided in my mind and in my loyalty?' Disturbed by such questions, he trudged along on foot till he emerged from the forest and presently came to a wide river.

It was late afternoon when he came to a bridge. A wooden house was built by the river bank, a wooden paling surrounding it, and within a fence a garden of herbs and vegetables.

Lancelot went wearily into the garden, to be greeted by a hermit, a brisk and capable man who had charge of ferrying travellers over the river. He was well-used to giving hospitality and warning travellers of dangers; for he knew very well where outlaws and robbers lay in wait in the depths of the forest.

'My friend' he said, 'you seem to be exhausted. Sit down and rest.' Lancelot drank gratefully from a clay jar of water that stood beside his bench.

'Tell me your name' said the hermit, 'and what brings you here.'

'My name is Lancelot of the Lake' he replied. 'I am one of the knights searching for the Grail.'

The hermit was astonished. 'You are the great Sir Lancelot?' he said. 'The King's right hand, the one who grew up in Avalon? Everyone knows about you. You have brought more fame to the Round Table than any other knight.'

He could hardly believe that the famous knight was sitting there, tired, dirty and footsore.

'None of that helps me now' said Lancelot. 'I am a most unhappy man. My fortunes have changed and all my skills have left me.'

The hermit was concerned to see his distress, and asked Lancelot what had happened. Lancelot told him everything: his fruitless search for the unknown knight who had felled him; the chapel he had been unable to enter; the accusing voice from the forest; and worst of all, his powerlessness when he had seen the Grail.

He would have gone on longer, but the hermit raised his hand and stopped him.

'You are the leader of King Arthur's knights' he said. 'To achieve that, God gave you more gifts than any of the others. Everyone knows that you have got strength, courage, understanding and good fortune. Now you say that these gifts have left you. There must be some reason.'

Lancelot did not reply.

The hermit said 'Is it because you have used these gifts for yourself or someone else, and not in God's service? It grieves me that so far your quest has failed; but believe me, unless God is your only Lord it will go on failing.'

Lancelot was still silent.

'You have not told me everything' the hermit said.

Lancelot had no wish to say more but the hermit urged him, saying 'How can I help you if you do not speak?'

In the end the hermit prevailed, so that Lancelot confessed and said:

'This is the way it is. For twenty years I have loved Queen Guinevere. All I ever did in war or peace was for her sake. It was never for the sake of God, but to win her love and faithfulness. I love the queen immeasurably. She watched over me when I first went to Camelot; she has brought me power and riches and used her influence for me. I owe her everything. All has gone well for us until this quest began. Now I see that I am a divided man. What must I do?'

The hermit was direct and plain.

'Unless you promise to avoid the queen, I cannot counsel you.'

Lancelot could not bring himself to accept these words. He said:

'I love the queen more than anyone else in this world, though she is the wife of the great man who is my lord. Without her my life would be nothing.'

The hermit cut him short.

'You are also a traitor to your lord King Arthur, and a danger to your whole fellowship. I assure you that so long as you are divided in your loyalty you can never hope to find the Grail.'

'As for those words you heard at the chapel' he continued, 'they are true enough, as your own words show. You are harder than stone, for water cannot enter stone and the Holy Spirit cannot enter you. You are more bitter than the bark that rots on a tree branch; you are fruitless like that fig which could give our Lord no fruit when he needed it.'

Seeing his despondency, the hermit invited Lancelot to stay with him. He was a practical, methodical man and had been a knight himself in earlier days. He was in charge of the bridge and the surrounding forest, and he ruled with a very strict rule. Lancelot was astonished to see swords and spears in the house.

'Do you see yourself as a knight or a hermit?' he asked one day, when the hermit had returned from an expedition into the forest in pursuit of some renegade.

He said 'I see myself as both. Have you never heard of Leofgar, who was bishop of Hereford in the old days? When folk were in danger he set aside his spiritual weapons and took his sword and spear and went out to protect them. He was killed on the battlefield, they say.'

'A knight can be a man of God as a hermit can?' said Lancelot.

The hermit looked at him, considering.

'I have heard about the new knights in the Holy Land' he said. 'Knights who live in Jerusalem near the Temple. Those men live like monks yet they fight and give their lives to protect Christian people in the holy places. Yes, I believe it is possible; any man can be a man of God.'

Lancelot remained with him until the autumn, and by then they had become friends. The hermit was well-known and respected throughout the district, and he was able to find a grey spotted horse for Lancelot, to say nothing of a helmet, a chain-mail coat, a lance and a shield. What is more, he himself set about reinforcing the second-hand shield and carefully repainted it with the wavy blue and white bands that indicated the Lake of Avalon where Lancelot had grown up. It was due more to the hermit's friendship and generosity than to his words that Lancelot rode away with gratitude and fresh resolve.

In the coming days he met many discouragements.

A passing cleric, quite unknown to him, halted in his walk and called to him 'I know who you are, Lancelot from Avalon. You are one of King Arthur's knights, hoping to see the Grail. Let me tell you, this is as likely as a blind man seeing the grass growing. Go back to Camelot.'

With these words he stepped back smartly into the priest's house and shut the door.

Lancelot was glad to get away before anyone else recognised him, but the next day he passed through a market and, by chance, fell in with the very squire who had seen him at the deserted chapel. They knew one another immediately

The youth pulled up his horse and said scornfully 'I never thought to see you again. You turned your back on the Grail, and the miracle it worked. You care nothing for the Grail, so be sure the Grail will care nothing for you. You will never find it. You might as well search for last year's snow. Anyway,' he added, 'it's not the Grail you want, it's Queen Guinevere!'

He laughed rudely and then rode off hastily, for he saw the fury on Lancelot's face.

After taunts like these he began to lose heart, but then one day he fell in with a devout lady who was making her way towards a Benedictine monastery for Vespers. They rode together, she on a tall white mule, while she told him of her great devotion to the monastery and its wonderful relics. She had her prayer book with her, a psalter bound together with the Little Hours of the Virgin; she was so proud of these that she reined in the mule to take the book out of its covering and show him some of the bright pages. The book had been written and illuminated by one of the monks, she said, and the sub-prior had arranged for the vellum pages to be bound up together.

Presently, she asked 'Where are you bound for?'

'Wherever God leads me' he replied. 'I am on a quest but I don't know where it will take me.'

'I know very well what you are seeking' she said. 'Listen now, there was once a time when you were very much closer to your goal than you are today; and yet, if you persevere, you will find yourself coming closer to it than you expect.'

He was still considering these words when they arrived at the church, where he helped her to dismount.

He stood and studied the main door over which masons had carved a whole company of saints, with Christ, Judge of the World at their centre. The stone had been painted red, green, blue and gold, and it shone nearly as brightly as the pages of the lady's prayer-book.

Lancelot remembered the words of the hermit, and rode away in a sober frame of mind. Then he took the path beside a narrow river fringed with reeds.

Before long the sky grew overcast and heavy rain began to fall. He rode through it unhappily, and he noticed that whilst the rain fell on his side of the river, the other side enjoyed the sun and was entirely dry. He could not understand it, so he called out to a young man who was fishing on the opposite bank.

'Tell me, friend' he said, 'why does it rain on this side of the river, but on your side not a drop?'

'Sir' answered the young man, 'you must have done something to deserve it. It is the sky showing you its displeasure.'

Next day he continued to follow the river and arrived at a fortified tower set beside a small thatched church built of wood.

Some sort of assembly had taken place in the church, and among the horses coming from the churchyard he suddenly recognised his own horse, Traveller, which had been stolen from him. He looked hard at the rider and recognised him as the injured knight who had been carried to the chapel. He looked well and cheerful enough now, and at the sight of him Lancelot's fury overwhelmed him. He rushed at him shouting 'Thief! This is for stealing my horse and armour!' swinging his sword so that the other bent under a rain of blows. Lancelot's double-edged sword cut through the man's defence and he fell from the saddle, a great dent in his helmet.

Lancelot left him lying there. He took back his own horse and left the other horse for the knight when he should regain his senses. He tied it to a tree overhanging the church wall.

During the following days Lancelot spoke to few people, except when he was given hospitality in an abbey of White monks. He had been here in past days and was well known to the prior. The whole monastery was full of activity, for it was autumn now and all the brothers and labourers were out in the monastery orchard. The cattle that normally grazed under the trees had been removed, and Lancelot watched the brothers beating the branches with long sticks till no fruit was left, raking up the crimson bittersharps and carting them off to be pressed. This monastery was famous for its cider which was sold as far away as Gloucester.

Lancelot would have dearly liked to prolong his stay among his friends, but he overrode his inclination and said goodbye. He had no idea in which direction to travel, and when he found himself at a place where four roads met in a green valley, he made up his mind. He said, 'Let God show me the right path.' He took his hands off the reins and said to Traveller: 'Go wherever you want to go.'

The horse made its way towards the west, and daylight faded as they rode. Just before sunset he found himself on a desolate hillside studded with rocky outcrops. Someone had planted a tall wooden cross among the rocks. Lancelot took off his helmet, unsaddled his horse to let it graze on the scanty grass, and

The Nine Stars in the Sky

lay down beside the cross. He thought about his friend the hermit-knight, he said the prayers he knew by heart, and then he fell asleep.

As he slept, he had a dream. In reality, the autumn sky was lowering and overcast but in his dream it was full of glittering stars. As he watched, nine of these stars moved across the sky and came down to light up the place where he lay. Out of their brightness, nine warriors emerged, and Lancelot knew with the certainty often found in dreams that two of them were knights and seven of them kings. They knelt and prayed together saying 'Father in heaven, come to us, repay us for what we have done in our lives.'

At this the night sky opened wide to reveal a man surrounded by angels. He came into their midst and greeted them in turn, blessing them, embracing them and saying 'You are my faithful knight; you are my loyal man.'

But when he came to the elder of the two knights, his face darkened.

'You are no friend of mine' he said. 'I gave more to you than any other knight and you have wasted it all. You have not lived to serve me but to please yourself, and to win money and fame. You promised your loyalty to me and you have given it to others.'

At this the knight cried out in grief and protest, but the man said 'It is for you to choose. You can be my friend or you can be my enemy.'

Then Lancelot lost sight of him, for the knight fled away. His eyes were riveted now on the second man, the young knight, because the man went up to him, kissed him and said:

'You will travel further than anyone. You will fly above the world.' And he changed the man's human shape and gave him wings so that he could fly. The young knight spread these wings and they took him high above them all, right among the stars, where he was lost to sight.

Next day when he thought about the dream, Lancelot had no idea what it might mean. 'I must find some hermit or some recluse who can tell me' he thought.

He met a man and woman and their family of six children, all hard at work picking fruit from the hedgerows, and he asked if they knew of any hermit in the district.

'Go right ahead, sir' said the man. 'Go to the church and you'll see a thatched house there; that's the hermit, that's our village.'

Lancelot rode ahead, and soon came to the church and a cluster of buildings. He examined the church, and saw a sundial cut into the stone and he realised that it was nearly three o'clock. He dismounted and looked for the thatched house. He was tired and hungry, too. When he saw a very old bent man with a basket of vegetables he guessed that this must be the hermit, so he asked him for food.

The old man led him to a wattle and daub shack with rotting thatching overhanging its one little window.

'I will give you whatever I have' he told Lancelot, 'and you can sleep here, too.'

After the horse was fed, they shared a meal of barley bread with stewed green peas. The hermit told Lancelot that he believed he was over ninety years of age, and that he still spent most of his time out of doors, collecting herbs for healing, and snakes, too. He showed Lancelot his forked stick for pinning snakes to the earth. He reckoned snake oil among his best medicines.

'But birch bark is good, too' he said. 'Put the wet bark on a wound and it will soon heal.'

It was nearly time for Vespers now, and the old man invited Lancelot to join him in the church. Only after Vespers did he ask him who he was and where he was going.

When he heard Lancelot's story, the old man felt compassion for him.

'I have heard of you and of the Lake of Avalon' he said. 'If you have travelled as far as this little place, God must surely be guiding you.'

Cheered by this, Lancelot said:

'When I was sleeping beside the cross on a hill not far from here, I had a strange dream. I need someone to tell me what it means.'

That evening he and the old hermit sat together until midnight, the hermit asking him many questions. Then he interpreted the dream, and Lancelot grew more and more amazed at what he heard. The hermit said 'The nine men you saw praying round the cross were nine generations of one family – your family. These generations go back to the days of Joseph of Arimathea, who brought the Grail to Glastonbury and later hid it away in Carbonek. You saw yourself and your son among them. The knight who was disloyal and who fled away from God was an image of yourself. The young knight who soared above the earth was an image of Galahad your son.'

Lancelot was thunderstruck. 'That was my son Galahad!' he cried. 'The best knight of all! The one who flew over the earth!'

The hermit said with some severity:

'Who should know better than you that he is your son. You and his mother Elaine were brought together by enchantment twenty years ago, when you were bewitched into thinking that Elaine was Guinevere the Queen.'

Lancelot was still astonished, not least by the hermit's knowledge of these things.

'You only saw Galahad as a child' the hermit went on. 'He was left with King Pelles when you and Elaine went away to live in the north country. You returned to Camelot and Elaine went back to her father, and you have never seen him since. He came indeed to Camelot but you did not recognise him.'

The old man paused and put a new piece of rush into the oil-lamp; it threw a pale light across the room, flickering with the draught that came in through the half-closed window.

'You should be proud of Galahad' he said. 'He is the one Merlin spoke about, the knight who will find the Grail and look into its depths. It is easier to look straight into the face of the sun than to do that.'

The Nine Stars in the Sky

After a pause Lancelot said 'Surely such a man will pray for his father; God will surely listen if he prays for me.'

The hermit was not so sanguine.

'Certainly he will pray for you. He is your son but don't imagine you can rest on his prayers. You must make your own if you are to be faithful to your resolve. And you ought to pray for the hermits and recluses you have met on your journey. Providence put them in your way. They have helped you onto the path of Jesus Christ; that path is as green and full of life as the very forest itself.'

From that meeting, Lancelot went away with true resolve. He took the road to the west and found himself entering a dark and shadowy forest. Before long the paths became overgrown tracks, narrow and often closed in by thickets. Time after time he had to retrace his steps and fight his way between overhanging branches. At long last he emerged to find himself in a valley with steep hills rising up on either side. These hills grew steadily more rocky, more precipitous. He rode on because he could see a river in the distance. When he came to it, he realised that it was fed by streams pouring down the rock face and that no one could possibly ride through it.

He drew rein and considered what to do. As he looked around, he was aware of a man riding towards him from the other bank. Lancelot was struck by the build of the horse, for it was as tall and heavy as any plough-horse, and its rider seemed far bigger than any ordinary man. Without hesitation horse and rider plunged into the river and, despite the force of the water, rode fast towards Lancelot. He was taken completely by surprise. The tall man was armed and he jammed his spear halfway up its shaft into Lancelot's horse. Traveller screamed, staggered and fell dead beneath him.

By the time Lancelot had struggled free of the horse and got to his feet again, his assailant had vanished. Lancelot was amazed. 'That must have been a demon in a man's shape' he said to himself, 'with a demon horse, as well.' He was disturbed, and he grieved also for Traveller who had been his companion in many sorties and journeys.

He looked around him at this threatening place. There was no bridge over the river, so far as he could see. He studied the rocky slopes on either hand; they were too steep to climb. He thought of the thick and labyrinthine forest, and knew that he could never find his way back through it. He had no horse now, no privileged position as a horseman. He was only a needy lost man, who had to go on his own feet like the village men and women he had met; like the poor family scouring the hedgerows to get food for the winter.

He sat there for a long time. 'I shall never find the Grail now' he thought. Then he remembered the hermits who had helped him; he remembered what they had told him. So he prayed to be shown the path; he asked God for a sign.

A Kind of Travelling

CHAPTER 5

The Dark Powers

While Parcival puts out to sea and Lancelot rejoices at the vision of the stars, Bors still rides alone, mindful of the knights' decision. He has even parted from his brother Lionel, who has always been his companion.

Bors' travels take him into a world of dangerous demonic forces, where he must make agonising, almost impossible choices. After a nearly fatal encounter with Lionel, he hears the voice that spoke to Parcival. It commands him to search out a ship on the sea coast. In that ship, he learns, Parcival is waiting for him.

As the year turned, many of the knights began to regret their decision to travel alone, and when by chance they met up with friends, they were only too glad to forget Nascien's warnings.

One man remembered, though, as he rode alone for weeks through woodland, over hills and deep valleys dotted with sheep. He was Bors of Ganis. He had good reason to wonder where his fellow knights might be, since one of them was his older brother Lionel. The two of them stood close to Arthur, and even closer to each other in family loyalty and affection. They had fought in Arthur's wars for twenty years, and had experience in every sort of martial encounter.

In the late summer, as Bors was riding through a forest of ancient oak trees, he caught up with an elderly Benedictine monk on a donkey. The two men got into conversation. The monk, who was far more garrulous than Bors, began a long story of how he was on a visit to one of the servants of the abbey.

'He was a turf-digger' he said, 'but he is old and can't do much work now, so I go to see him from time to time.'

They left the forest track and rode across miles of flat land cut through with dikes. Presently they passed peat-workings and came to a tiny hut thatched with furze and bracken. The old peat-digger was painfully building a turf rick, aided by two little boys. He was bent and crippled but he and the monk greeted each other as old friends, and the monk left him with a sack of food.

Bors and the monk rode on companionably, and presently Bors explained that he was one of Arthur's knights and was searching for the Grail.

At this the monk pulled up his donkey and his cheerful face hardened.

'I have heard about this quest' he said. 'Our abbot told us about it in Chapter. He said that many of the knights should never have started on it, and I agree with him. Most of these men don't know what they are doing. They will go back empty-handed to Camelot, if they don't destroy themselves first. But what about you, my friend? Are you serious about this undertaking?'

'Sir,' said Bors, 'I strongly believe that this quest must be taken seriously, though I don't know where it will lead me or what the outcome will be. It has to do with mysteries we cannot understand.'

'Who are you?' asked the monk.

'I am a son of King Bors of Ganis' said Bors. 'My mother was Queen Evaine, and I have an older brother Lionel.'

At this the old monk laughed aloud and said:

'Believe it or not but I once met your father. My abbot sent me on a mission to Normandy, and your father visited our abbey there. He was the best Christian man I ever heard of, and everyone knows that your mother was a holy woman. With such good parents, the two of you should become holy men. Good trees can only produce good fruit.'

Bors disagreed.

'A man can have good parents and not be good; it depends on his own heart. A knight is not noble because his family is noble; his heart must be noble, too.'

The monk was surprised to hear this.

'It is very unusual for a layman to think about such things' he said. 'This is the province of monks and clerics.'

Bors did not reveal that he often thought about goodness and evil, and about the mystery of the God who cannot be seen but is present in the world. Indeed, he had once read a meditation by the Cistercian monk Bernard of Clairvaux, and had been stirred by it. For Bernard had written:

'God gave you life so you could respond to him; he shaped you so that you long for him, and he made you able to receive him.'

Bors had half understood what this meant, and the words simultaneously raised his heart and saddened him, for he could not fully believe that they were meant for him. He guessed that the old monk, too, would find them more suitable for clerics and religious than for layfolk. So he rode on in silence, the monk meanwhile describing in detail the new and wonderful decorations in his monastery church. He was still enthusing over the gold relic-cases and the silver lamps when they came to the pilgrims' hostel where he planned to stay.

Early next morning the priest who ran the hospice said Mass while Bors and a handful of pilgrims stood at the back of the chapel. A solid painted rood screen cut the nave from the sanctuary so that Bors could see nothing and hear nothing. As he had done for years, he stood upright and dutiful and said what prayers he knew; and he wondered not for the first time what secrets might lie behind the separating screen and why they were kept hidden.

Later that day the monk asked Bors if he would make a solemn promise before they parted. Bors hesitated. He would not commit himself till he knew what the promise entailed.

'Prove that you are steadfast in this quest of yours' said the monk. 'Promise that you will eat only bread and water until the day you sit down at the table of the Grail.'

Bors hesitated even more.

'Who knows that I shall ever do that?' he asked.

'I am certain of it' said the monk. 'Believe me, Bors. You will find the Grail one day; you and a few others, but not many of you.'

Then Bors promised, and before they went their separate ways the monk obtained a good supply of barley bread from the hermitage and presented it to Bors.

'This will remind you of your promise' he told him.

It was barely daybreak next day when Bors rode through the early morning mists, but the sun soon burned them off as the day grew warmer.

By midday he was hot and hungry. He drew rein, dismounted and sat with his back against the wall of a half-ruined sheep pound. The surrounding terrain was all rough moorland now, with dry stone walls running down the side of the valley he would have to descend.

While he was eating the barley bread, he noticed below him a stunted solitary leafless tree with a nest in its branches. A large grey bird was circling the nest. Bors stood up and looked at the nest which was full of young birds. This surprised him, for it was autumn, when all the young should be fledged. He looked again, then he realised that all these young birds were dead.

The grey bird flew around the nest again, then she flew closer and settled herself on the nest. Bors watched as she pierced herself with her beak so that her blood flowed over the chicks. To his astonishment they came back to life again; but as they chirped and cried and flexed their little wings, the grey bird drooped, sank down and died among them.

Bors stood for a long time and watched, but the bird did not stir. At length he took his horse and rode slowly on. He was convinced that there was some meaning in what he had just witnessed, but what this was he could not imagine.

That evening, when he came to a large village, he asked for lodging in the manor house. He was readily received by its lady, an elderly widow who remembered Bors from some distant gathering in Camelot which she and her husband had attended. They sat companionably together and played chess after dinner, sitting near a good log fire for the days were drawing in now.

She was curious about his quest and enquired after several of the knights whom she knew, notably Lancelot, Hector and Gawain. But he could tell her nothing of their progress.

Some days later he found himself riding towards a square stone tower, surrounded by broad meadowland and farms. Many people were assembled on the path, and as he rode closer they began to call out to him in anxious fearful voices.

'Sir, have you been sent to help us? Sir, what can we do? We shall all be ruined. Our lady will be destroyed.'

'What is wrong?' he asked, and any number of voices tried to tell him.

Then Bors turned to a man who looked like a forester, for some explanation.

'This tower belongs to the lady we serve' said the man. 'So does all the land you can see as far as those hills. But her sister has turned against our lady. She is bringing an army to take the tower and all the lands, and to destroy us.'

'Why should one sister make war upon another?' Bors said. 'They should be allies.'

The forester shook his head.

'The elder sister of our lady was married to the lord of this region. When he went off to the wars, he left her the castles, the land, and the loyalty of all his knights; but while he was absent, she set up a reign of terror with a pack of freelance knights so that none of us was safe, rich or poor. Then one day her lord returned. When he saw this, he took back everything from her and gave it to the younger sister; that is, to our lady. But now she is recently widowed, and so the elder sister is bringing an army against her. She is on her way now to take the tower.'

When he heard this Bors rode to the gate and asked for hospitality. The gate was opened, his horse taken, and he was led inside to be welcomed by the younger sister, the widow, who was plainly full of anxiety.

'Have you no one to fight for your claim?' Bors asked, when she repeated the story of her elder sister's enmity.

'I have only a few knights here' she said. 'They are all old men. None of them could fight for me; and yesterday I heard that my sister has got a champion in Sir Pridian.'

'Who might he be?' said Bors, for he had never heard of the man.

'He is the hardest, most merciless knight who ever lived in these parts. No one has ever beaten him, and everyone goes in fear of him. He is called the Black Warrior because all his armour is black, and his pennant as well.'

At this Bors made up his mind.

He said 'Tell your knights that I will fight this Pridian for you, to get you justice.'

The younger sister's spirits soared when she heard these words, and straightaway arrangements were made for the encounter to be held next morning.

To the handful of elderly knights Bors said:

'Your lady has justice on her side, and I am going to prove it. If I win tomorrow, all the countryside will know that her sister's claim is false.'

They gave Bors a semi-circular room to sleep in, with plenty of wax candles burning and a better bed than he had met since starting on the quest. First he prayed for God's help in the coming fight. Then he fell asleep, and as the night passed he dreamed the strangest dream.

He saw himself entering a large building, on one side of which was a man sitting on a throne. On the other side a decaying tree trunk grew out of the tiled floor. On either side of the tree two young plants were growing, each with a single flower: one straight, one bending towards the other. The man came from his throne and parted the two flowers, and as Bors watched he saw both these plants grow to become good young trees that produced flowers and fruit in abundance. In the dream the man asked Bors 'Which of these would you save? The rotten trunk or the flowering trees?'

'Oh, the trees' said Bors.

'Remember that answer' said the man, 'and be sure you put the trees first.'

So he awoke puzzled, having no idea what this dream might signify.

Very early next day Bors accompanied the widowed lady and rode out with her veteran knights into one of the surrounding meadows. Flags and pennants were flying, and all the towns-people and villagers had grouped themselves round the edges.

At the far end the elder sister sat on her grey mule, her knights behind her, Pridian at her side. On his black shield a boar's head was painted in gold.

Bors had never encountered that shield; nor was Pridian familiar with Bors' blue shield with its single silver star.

When Pridian, who was mounted on an aggressive skewbald horse, saw Bors, he left his men and rode about the field imperiously shouting threats:

'Tell your champion to come out if he dares! Who is this coward facing me?'

Bors rode on steadily.

'I am the lady's champion' he said, 'and I will prove her right to this tower and this land.'

With that, they rode furiously towards each other. Despite the protection given by the high saddle bows, each knight was swept from his horse. Both lances were broken and both men catapulted on to the grass. Scrambling to their feet, they set about each other with swords. They fought grimly, their double-edged swords tearing through chain-mail.

Then suddenly Bors flung himself at Pridian and fell on him, gripping him round the neck.

'Surrender if you want to live!' he shouted.

Pridian refused and tore himself free. Again they snatched up their swords, but now Bors had got the measure of his foe. He let Pridian take the initiative until he sensed that he was exhausted. At that point Bors attacked with such strength that Pridian tripped and fell backwards.

In a flash Bors was on him. He dragged off his helmet and threatened to behead him unless Pridian acknowledged the rights of the younger sister.

A Kind of Travelling

The Black Warrior fought for time, but Bors was inflexible. Pridian was forced to ask for mercy.

Bors' arm was cut in half-a-dozen places, his head rang from the blows on his helmet, and his face ran with sweat and rust from his armour. They got him back into the tower with speed, and set about dressing his wounds with ointment of yarrow leaves. He recovered within days, and made little of his wounds.

While he remained in the castle he used the time to enforce the authority of the younger sister all across the land. She would have been happy had he stayed longer, had he accepted reward for all he had done; but Bors told her about his quest and he went on his way, to the thanks and cheers of all the people.

He rode back into the forest, down a bridle path. He thought he would recognise the way he had come, but it seemed strangely different so that he was uncertain which way to go. The path branched into half-a-dozen shady tracks and he chose one at random.

After a time this track came to a crossroads and here to his amazement he saw his brother Lionel, bound hand and foot and slung across the back of a mule, while two men beat him with thorny branches.

Bors was filled with rage, and he spurred on his horse, his sword ready in his hand. An instant later he heard the thudding of hooves and a woman's screams as a horse galloped into the clearing.

'Help me! Help me!' she was crying, struggling against the armed man who held her before him in the saddle.

'Help me! You are a knight. Rescue me from this man! Mother of God, listen to me!'

Bors was horrified, appalled by the choice that faced him.

'God, what must I do?' he thought. 'Save Lionel from death, or this girl from rape?'

He paused, bewildered. Suddenly, he made up his mind and said:

'I must save the girl, and may God protect my brother.'

Meanwhile the horseman held the girl more grimly and made to ride off with her into the thicker part of the forest. Bors rode after him furiously. Then the man flung the girl from the saddle and turned to fight. He and Bors met with a great collision, falling together on to the forest floor. They got to their feet and set about each other with swords, but it was not long before Bors had cut through the man's armour into his shoulder so that his blood poured out among the ferns, and he fainted away.

Bors turned to the girl. 'You are free' he said. 'What do you want of me now?'

'Oh, to go back to my father's house' she said.

So he set her on the horse of the fallen knight and took her home. Her brothers, in gratitude, tried to make him stay and to accept reward but he was not to be persuaded. His thoughts were all for Lionel. He rode back to search for his brother, but there was no sign of him or his captors. Finding no one, he followed the path down which Lionel had been taken.

The Dark Powers

The whole forest seemed silent and motionless, with no sound of a human voice nor of a bird. The skies darkened to a purple colour and the leaves shone with a sinister green light. He could feel his horse's fear and he himself was deeply uneasy. The shadowy track he was following grew darker and more difficult, beset by fallen trees half hidden among the ferns, all decaying into the soil. The silence was so melancholy that he was greatly relieved to reach open land again, and to find ahead of him a man in priest's clothing, riding a bay horse. He halted and asked Bors where he was bound for.

'My brother has been captured by two men' said Bors. 'I am trying to find him.'

The man shook his head. 'I know about your brother, my dear friend. I have got news for you, but it is bad news full of sorrow.'

Bors narrowed his eyes.

'How do you know this?' he asked. There was some quality in the priest that disturbed him.

'Look there' said the priest, pointing. Bors was filled with foreboding as he looked, for there in a thicket lay the body of his brother

At this Bors was too much overcome with grief to say a word. He slid from his horse, fell on his knees, brushed the earth from Lionel's face and took him up in his arms, noticing with fear that his body seemed to have no more weight than a child's.

Then he placed Lionel across the saddle of his horse and followed the priest, who led him to a derelict stone building half overgrown with thorn trees. Within it was a stone slab, and here they laid Lionel. The place had no cross, no bell, no window, no altar, only the stone slab.

'This is no Christian chapel' said Bors, but the priest reassured him and promised that the next day he would return to bury Lionel with all the rites of the Church.

'Meanwhile' he told Bors, 'follow me. We must press on to the Moorland Castle' and he pointed to the West where Bors could see a splendid stone castle with four high towers set among tall trees, a river flowing beside it.

'We can be sure of friends there' the priest said. 'The castle is ruled by a lady, a woman with great power. She has every human gift, and she is beautiful as well. I have stayed there many times.'

Meanwhile Bors had been studying this priest, whom he did not entirely trust. He asked him 'You are a priest, a Christian priest?'

'Certainly I am; you can put all your confidence in me.'

As they rode along, Bors decided to confide in the priest. He was anxious in his mind about his decision to desert Lionel. He was shocked and dismayed when the priest said 'Your decision was wrong. You should have rescued your brother. You left him to pain and death, and went to the rescue of some useless girl who means nothing to you. She had no claims on you, but your brother had. You deserted him and now you have caused his death. Do you understand?'

'I understand' said Bors, and the two rode on in silence.

Presently the priest spoke again.

'There is more to it than that' he said. 'When your family hear how you have acted, it will cause dissension among them because some will be for you and some against you. More deaths will follow in your family as a result, and you will be responsible for them as well.'

Bors thoughts were still in turmoil when they came to the castle and were presently led into its great hall. This was a far grander castle than Camelot, with many clear glass windows, and floors flagged with blue and green stone. Everywhere Bors looked he saw paintings on the stone walls. The doors were made of polished wood, with golden hinges; and everywhere lights were burning and they, too, were set in golden candlesticks.

They were greeted by the lady's chamberlain who said to Bors:

'Sir, we knew from signs in the sky that you would come here on this very day. Our lady is expecting you. She is in love with you already, before she even sees you. She will ask you to promise allegiance to her, and this is the greatest honour she could give you.'

They led Bors to an upper room bright with candles, where they gave him a blue woollen robe and shoes of Spanish leather. As he removed his armour he wondered how he could get away from this place, but he had little opportunity to make any plans. The lady of the castle and three of her attendants appeared, inviting him to dinner. They were so pressing, so warm hearted in their welcome, that his apprehensions subsided and presently he sat at table with them.

Before the end of the meal, the chamberlain said to Bors: 'Our lady, our ruler of all these lands, asks you to pledge yourself to her, to stay with her as her lord and lover.'

The lady then said to Bors: 'See, I am wearing your colours.'

She raised her arms, and he saw that her long sleeves were made of blue silk decorated with silver stars, exactly like the one on his shield. All her ladies were wearing the same emblem.

'I entreat you to stay with me' she urged Bors. 'I will give you the lordship of the castle. I have waited a long time for you to come.'

Taking him by the arm, she drew him to one of the windows which looked out over meadows and woodland, and far away to the sea.

'All this will be yours' she said, 'if you will give me your allegiance and stay with me.'

Bors was taken aback. He had no wish to stay, and the thought of Lionel's fate rose up in his mind. He refused, explaining that he could not give up the quest he had sworn to follow.

At this, the lady began to weep. She implored him to remain. 'My dearest, dearest friend, I beg of you. I will give you anything you ask.'

But when he remained steadfast, she grew angry and said 'If you will not stay with me, my life is useless. I will kill myself before your very eyes. Yes, I will throw myself down from the top of the tower with all my ladies.'

She called twelve of her ladies up the stone stairway to the battlements.

'She will never do such a thing' Bors said within himself, as he and everyone else crowded into the courtyard and looked up at them.

One of the women shouted:

'Oh Bors, do what our lady asks of you! If you refuse, we shall throw ourselves down, and you will be responsible. Where is your honour? Do you want to cause our deaths? You are a Christian knight. You must preserve life, not destroy it.'

Bors watched as they hovered above him on the battlements. He found them pitiful, and he would have helped them if he could but he had made up his mind.

'I will not stay!' he cried.

At that all the women screamed and flung themselves down onto the stones of the courtyard below.

Bors was horrified beyond words.

'God, help me! What should I have done?' he thought.

He crossed himself and as he did so, red hot embers rained down from the sky, the broken bodies of the women turned to ashes, and from the ashes a flock of black ravens rose and vanished into the sky. Nothing was left standing except the bare blackened walls of the castle, while every tree was snapped off to its roots. Bors was the only one left alive. He looked round the desolate ruin. The only familiar sight was his horse waiting there, his sword, shield and lance lying beside it.

'For God's sake, let me get away from here' he thought, furiously rearming himself.

He rode far away until he came to high stone walls with a wide gate. Within was a newly-built Cistercian monastery; and behind it, fields of barley and rye stretching almost to the edge of a forest. He asked for shelter and for the services of some monk who could counsel him.

Next day the abbot led Bors out into an enclosed garden used as a burying place for the monks. It was peaceful, with a plain wooden cross, and grass growing on all the graves.

Bors told the abbot the whole story of his quest, and the monk listened with concentration, looking up at him from time to time.

When the tale was finished, the abbot said:

'It seems to me that God has certainly marked you out to achieve something in this quest. You have been tempted all the time by devils who could see your weaknesses. These devils are the creatures that fell from heaven and now wander round the world deceiving many a good man like yourself. That priest you met was no priest, and his advice was only meant to put confusion in your mind. The women in the castle were all phantoms; dark powers all bent on deceiving you and weakening your resolve.'

Bors said 'What of the bird I saw that died in the nest?'

'That was a vision from God' said the abbot. 'What you saw was this world in the shape of the withered tree, and the Lord Jesus Christ in the shape of the grey bird. When she flew to her chicks, the bird found them dead; and the tree lifeless, too. So she settled on the nest and struck herself with her beak so that her blood flowed over them. She died on the nest but the young birds got life from her sacrifice. Had you been there later, you might have seen the tree grow green and full of sap again, because the Lord is the rescuer of the whole creation and loves it all.'

'I wish I understood these things' said Bors after a pause, 'but my life is taken up more with wars and travelling than with books.'

The abbot laughed, as if he found this amusing. He said 'Our father Bernard says that wisdom comes from many sources, not only books. I have seen a letter of his which might have been written for you, for he says:

"I know from experience that you will find something more in the forests than you do in books. The rocks and the trees will teach you what you cannot learn from masters."

'So' the abbot said, looking hard at Bors, 'believe me, everything you meet on this quest of yours and everything that happens, is God telling you about himself. He moves in all things; he is their very root.'

Then the monk went on to speak of Lionel.

'Your brother is still alive, and you are going to meet him again. What you do not realise, however, is that he is no true, honest knight. Remember your dream of the rotten tree trunk. Lionel is like that, without goodness or green leaves.'

This was a hard thing to have to listen to, for Bors loved his brother.

The abbot went on.

'You saw your brother – that rotten tree trunk – and in front of it, two plants. Now this will surprise you. One of these plants was an image of the girl you rescued in the forest; the other, an image of the knight who tried to rape her. The gardener who kept the plants apart was you yourself. Now in your dream, those plants had only one flower apiece to begin with but you saw them grow and send out leaves and more shoots and flowers, and finally many fruits. This is to tell you that both these two made good lives afterwards. Both had children and grandchildren, all good Christian people, and it was you who helped to bring it about. What you did on that day will have results far beyond anything you can imagine.'

Bors did not reflect deeply on all this; his thoughts were all for Lionel's welfare. He asked 'Do you know where my brother is? I must find him before I go on further.'

'You will find him at a tournament beyond the river' the abbot said. 'Cross the river at the ford, take the path up the hills into the next valley, and at the very edge of the valley you will see the castle. There are broad meadows surrounding it.'

Following these directions, Bors rode on slowly, thinking about Lionel.

He came upon the meadows and saw the preparations being made for the tournament: the pavilions, the horses, the gathering of knights and squires, the business of the castle, the serfs and servants hard at work.

Alongside the meadow was a hermit's house, and a horse tethered to a railing. Bors recognised the horse. It was Lionel's. At that moment, he saw his brother sitting outside the hermit's door. With a great shout of joy, he rode to him, slid off his horse and held out his arms.

But Lionel flung him off.

'Traitor! False brother! Coward! You preferred some unknown girl to me. You have shamed our whole family. Get out of here, or I will kill you on the spot!'

Bors fell down on his knees and tried to explain, but Lionel shouted:

'You deserted me, your brother! Let me get my lance and I will kill you now!' He rushed towards the horse, got his weapon and rode towards his brother. Bors thought 'I cannot fight him, and he must not fight me.'

He did not know what to do. So he knelt in front of Lionel and cried again: 'Brothers must not fight!'

But Lionel rode at him and trampled him underfoot. Bors lay there so battered and destroyed that he thought he would die. Now the hermit heard this shouting, and he ran forward, attempting to hold Lionel back, for he had dismounted and was dragging Bors' helmet off so as to behead him. The hermit thrust himself between the two and Lionel killed him with a single slash of his sword.

Another of Arthur's knights witnessed this murder and rushed to help the wounded Bors. He was an old man but active still, and he seized Lionel by the neck and hauled him back.

At this, Lionel turned on him with his sword and the two fought on and on, till Bors came back to his senses.

The old man was weakening now and he cried to Bors for help, but Bors could barely stand. Lionel slashed again, and now the old knight fell, his head struck from his shoulders.

At this Bors made a tremendous effort and took his sword. He cried 'I do not want to fight you but I have no choice.'

He had hardly spoken when Lionel's sword struck his. At the moment the blades met, a sheet of flame flashed from the sky, ran down their sword blades in green and blue flames and felled them both, blackening their shields, burning and charring the grass and all the trees.

Not one of the onlookers dared move, but after a long while all those present heard a clear voice say:

'Bors, leave your brother. Do not travel with him again. Get away from this place and make for the sea.'

Bors got up from the blackened ground. He was amazed to find his wounds healed. He asked Lionel to forgive him and his brother said:

'As God forgives you, so do I; and I ask your forgiveness.'

So they embraced each other, and Lionel promised to bury the two men he had killed. He kept his word and had them buried with great honour inside the church nearby; and he left a good sum of money to pay for candles to burn beside the tombs, and for a mason to carve their names.

Bors rode away, thanking God that Lionel and he were at peace again. He travelled for days and nights, asking anyone he met to direct him to the sea.

Eventually he found the path and rode along grassy cliff-tops patterned with sheep tracks. Below were little sandy bays and an occasional fisherman's chapel built into the cliffs. He spent one night with a small company of monks who had a farm there; and during the night he heard the same voice that had spoken to him at the tournament.

'Take your horse and go out secretly' it said. 'Follow the road till you see a white ship on the sea. Parcival is waiting for you.'

Dawn had not broken when he found the ship in one of the bays. He could see the white sail in the darkness. He left his horse on the sand amid the rock pools, and splashed through the shallow water, shouting as he ran.

Parcival recognised his voice immediately. Bors heaved himself into the ship and set down his lance and sword. The two embraced each other and laughed at the strangeness of their meeting. They stared at one another in wonder, saying over and over:

'What happened to you in all these months? Where did you travel? Who did you meet?'

At last Bors asked 'Did you ever think our quest would lead us to the sea?'

'Never, but maybe Carbonek is by the sea' said Parcival. 'We may be near the goal. Galahad would know.'

'All we lack now is Galahad' said Bors, 'but who knows where this quest has taken him.'

Their ship sailed out among the fishermen in the bay, and the sun rose and lighted up the sky.

CHAPTER 6

A Kind of Knowledge

From now onwards the journeys of Parcival, Bors, Lancelot and Galahad will meet, overlap, divide and reunite in a constantly shifting pattern.

When Galahad, who has been riding alone, seeks hospitality from a hermit, he is approached by a total stranger, a young woman determined to join in the quest. She leads Galahad on a demanding journey to the sea coast, to the very ship where Bors and Parcival have already met. This new member of their group is Dindrane. The men find that she understands more about the Grail than they do and they accept her teaching. She brings generosity, initiative and a deep wisdom to the group and this makes her their virtual leader right up to her death.

By now it was well into autumn, and the rains fell and the nights grew longer. One evening as he rode between the dripping trees, Galahad saw a thread of smoke rising ahead of him. He pushed on and came upon a hermitage. It seemed newly-established, for both house and chapel were built of clean wood and thatched with reeds. They stood on meadowland and a river ran nearby swollen with the rain, dangerously high.

The elderly hermit opened a window, greeted Galahad and stabled his horse. Within the house he cleared away slivers of wood from a bench where he had been working. He carved spoons from the white wood of the nearby elder trees, he told Galahad. Presently they were sitting beside a tiny fire sharing the hermit's supper, which was a porridge made from bread mashed with elderberries. Galahad told him about his quest, the strange events he had witnessed and the places he had visited. The old man asked him many questions. He had himself encountered several of the knights riding on their journeys but he could not identify any of them.

'One or two seemed determined on their quest' he said, 'as I see you are; but some had no heart for it.'

Presently the hermit brought in a good heap of dried grass and spread it out for Galahad, who soon settled down and fell into a deep sleep.

In the middle of the night, there was a repeated knocking on the door. The hermit opened the window, thinking it might be a request for his assistance. He was surprised to see a young woman standing there in the moonlight, holding the reins of a grey horse. She called up to him

'Sir Ulphin, I have a message for the knight who is staying with you. It is urgent, I must speak with him.'

Meanwhile Galahad was still asleep. The hermit went to rouse him.

'There is a young woman outside who says she must speak to you' he said.

Galahad was astonished. 'Who is she?' he asked. 'No one knows that I am here.'

The hermit said 'She hasn't told me her name but she seems determined to speak to you. I must say she has chosen a strange time for such a visit' and his face took on a guarded and suspicious look as he unbolted the door.

Galahad got up from his bed of straw and went out to speak to his visitor. He had no idea who she was nor what she wanted from him, and he was surprised by her composure as she stood before him.

'Galahad,' she said, 'I want you to arm yourself, to harness your horse and ride with me. If you do so, I promise that providence will show us both the greatest marvels that anyone could pray for.'

She spoke with such conviction that he instantly believed her. Without hesitation he went back into the house, put on his armour, saddled his horse and slung his red and white shield across his back.

He thanked the hermit for his hospitality, and asked for his prayers; and the young woman begged the priest's pardon for having disturbed him. The old man made light of it.

'God bless you' he said, 'and bring you both to what you are seeking, no matter how far the journey takes you.'

'Lead on and I will follow you' said Galahad, never thinking how strange it was for her to lead and for him to follow. They rode for the rest of that night and all the following day, over wild moorland with outcrops of rock, and here and there relics of old lead mines.

He noticed that she rode as well as he did, and that she was quite certain of their direction. They rode in silence under a thin moon.

Presently they halted. Ahead of them, standing on a hill was a castle, not large but well fortified and nearly encircled by the arm of a river.

'We are bound for that castle' she said.

He asked 'Is that your home?'

'It is where I have lived since I was a child' she replied, 'though the lady is not my mother, but a friend of hers. Our lord Edmund is away in the wars in Jerusalem, and she rules the castle. She has given me her permission to ride with you.'

'I do not even know your name' he said, and she told him.

'I am called Dindrane. My mother's name was Ashfleur.'

Then she asked 'Do you remember Nescien the hermit, the preacher who took you to King Arthur's court? Each year he visits our lady here. She is glad to get his counsel, for she has to manage all the affairs of the castle. She is a wise woman and she looks to all the buying and selling and the harvesting of the crops. She gives judgement in disputes and makes sure that peace reigns throughout her lands. Nescien is her friend, as he is mine. He has told me that the Grail is hidden in Castle Carbonek and that all King Arthur's knights have sworn to find it. Now I am going with you.'

By evening they had reached the castle, where they were welcomed in the courtyard by a group of men with lighted torches in their hands.

'Do we sleep here tonight?' asked Galahad eagerly, for he was wearied with riding.

'We eat first, and then sleep' she told him.

He imagined that they would leave late next day, but it was still dark when they awakened him and the sun had barely risen when he and Dindrane were on their way again with fresh horses.

As they rode, he asked her 'How did you know my name, and how did you know where to find me?'

She said simply 'It was shown to me. I know that you are seeking the Grail. I know that three of you will find it; and I know I have some part in that search, though not to its end.'

He did not understand but he kept silent and accepted what she said. He noticed, too, that she had brought with her a small box of birchwood which she secured on the pommel of her saddle.

Again they rode on, and the path took them westwards until they came to sand dunes and the sea itself. Below in a shingly bay they could see a white-sailed ship tied up to a wooden jetty, and nearby two knights walking on the wet sand.

'Are we to go on board?' asked Galahad.

Like all the knights he feared the sea, where the strength of men and horses counted for little and which no king or ruler could command.

Dindrane did not seem to share these apprehensions, for when they had dismounted she said to him: 'Take your shield and lance but let us leave the horses.'

She then led him over the sand. The horses looked after them doubtfully and wandered away. The two knights waved and shouted, and Galahad recognised them at once as Parcival and Bors. He shouted greetings in return, and in no time the three of them were embracing, cheering and celebrating this reunion. Each outdid the others in retelling all that had happened to him since the beginning of the quest.

'What a miracle!' cried Parcival. 'Did you ever think we would all meet again on a ship!'

They laughed aloud, and would have continued their rejoicing indefinitely had Bors not realised that Dindrane was standing silent and alone at the edge of the water, her wooden box in her hands.

He said 'Here we are, forever talking about our own concerns, and we do not know who this lady is, nor what brings her here.'

'I know!' cried Galahad. 'Forgive me, I should have told you at once. This is Dindrane. It is due to her that we have met. I would never have ridden in this direction but for her guidance. You must thank her for our meeting.'

When they had greeted Dindrane, they all went into the ship. The tide was ebbing, and a moderate wind rose which took them out to sea.

After a time Parcival said 'I am in mortal fear of this ocean.'

'This isn't the ocean' said Bors. 'This is the Severn Sea. I have sailed on it before with King Arthur.'

'But aren't you afraid of where it may take us? We may come to the edge of the world and get swept up in the Circling Ocean. Then we can never come back.'

They were all uneasy. Parcival said 'I am not made for this trackless sea. If I ride on land I can go where I choose, but here it is the sea that rules and takes us with it. Have you ever heard of anyone who could command the sea?'

Dindrane said 'The holy man Brendan went on the ocean and trusted it, and he found the Islands of the Blessed at the end of it.'

'Yes' said Parcival, 'and he found terrifying things as well: islands made of sharp glass, rocks that moved with the currents, and sea monsters.'

'He also found trees full of fruit like jewels, and holy men living at peace with one another. He came back from his voyage and told his story. So' she said, 'one of us will go back to Camelot in the end, and tell them how we entrusted ourselves to the sea, and where it took us.'

They wondered how she came by this knowledge, and why she spoke with such authority.

Next day, the wind took their ship to a steep island with flocks of birds on its rocky stacks. There was a passageway through to a rough harbour, and here they saw another ship moored, a ship larger than their own and of quite different construction.

Dindrane told them 'We must go into that ship.'

None of them questioned her decision, and they made their way together towards it.

The ship left them dumbfounded. It was no working vessel like their own half-decked broad-beamed sturdy ship. In the first place, it was totally deserted; in the second, it bore no evidence of having sailed on any sea! No marks of salt or wind disfigured it, no tar covered the timbers or the crow's nest at its masthead. Its sail was pure white linen, embroidered with interlocking purple and scarlet rings.

They stood looking into it, uncertain and mystified. Suddenly Bors saw some writing on the ship's side. He drew attention to it and they all read these words:

'DO NOT GO INTO THIS SHIP UNLESS YOU HAVE FAITH. IF YOU DISOBEY, YOUR LIFE WILL BRING NOTHING BUT MISFORTUNE.'

A Kind of Knowledge

They stared in perplexity, no one wanting to go on board. Then out of the silence, Dindrane said to Parcival 'Do you know me, Parcival?'

'Why, no' he said, 'I never saw you until yesterday.'

'You do not remember me' she went on, 'but I am your sister. You are my youngest brother. Our mother took you to the Snow Mountains of Wales when our father King Pellinore was killed and all her land was taken from her. She left me in the Castle on the Mount where I still live, and where I took Galahad on our way here.'

Parcival stared at her, too amazed to speak.

'I am telling you this' said Dindrane, 'so that you will all trust me in whatever happens to us.'

They grew more confident then, and went into the ship, exclaiming at the strangeness of it. In the centre part a bed had been built with a canopy above it. The canopy and its supports were built of the strangest wood: white, green and red; not painted, but clearly the natural colour of the trees.

A sword lay across the bed, the blade half-drawn from the rose-red scabbard. The sword-belt was a poor tawdry thing of hemp, quite unsuited to the scabbard or to the sword-hilt, which was carved from walrus ivory and inlaid with gemstones. As they fixed their eyes on the sword, they saw a movement along the scabbard, and letters appeared creating these words:

'NO ONE HAS EVER BEEN ABLE TO GRIP ME, AND ONLY ONE HAND SHALL DO SO.'

Immediately, Parcival reached out and tried to grip the hilt but it was too large for him. Bors followed, and his attempt was no more successful. Galahad did not try, because he was still watching the scabbard, where new words were forming:

'LET NO ONE BE ARROGANT ENOUGH TO DRAW THIS SWORD. WHOEVER ATTEMPTS IT IS DOOMED TO DESTRUCTION UNLESS HE IS THE MOST STEADFAST KNIGHT OF ALL.'

They stood in awe before this warning, not knowing what to do. Then Dindrane said:

'There was one knight to whom the words do not apply, but before I tell you his name you must listen to the story of this ship. It will make things clearer to you.'

She indicated the supports of the canopy with their strange colours.

'All that wood came from a tree in the Garden of Eden' she said. 'When Adam and Eve were expelled, Eve took a twig with her and planted it to remind her of happier times. It grew and flourished, and all its wood and leaves were white as snow. Adam said that it was a tree of death, but Eve disagreed.

"Not so" she told him, "it is far better called the Tree of Life because one day joy will come into the world because of it."

'Time passed, and when Eve gave birth to Abel the white tree changed into green and began to grow flowers and fruit, which it had never done before. It remained green, as did all the cuttings they took from it, until the day when Abel was killed by Cain his brother. At that hour the green leaves turned scarlet in memory of the suffering and the bloodshed.

From that time onwards the tree neither aged nor withered. It survived the flood when water covered the earth, and so did all the trees descended from it. Even in the time of King Solomon, the trees were still full of life and vigour.'

They all stared at the age-old wood, and Parcival ran his hands down the green column. It was smooth as an adze could make it, and he could see the grain of the wood bright as emerald.

Dindrane went on:

'This ship belonged to King Solomon. He was the wisest man who ever lived and he knew everything that can be known. One day when studying an ancient writing, he learned that he would have many descendants, the last of whom would achieve great things. He saw this man in a dream, and the man was sleeping in a ship. Solomon told this to his wife and between them they set out to build a ship – this very ship – believing that it would sail the seas until in years to come this man would find it. Since the ship was going to sail into the future, Solomon's wife insisted that it should bring the past with it. So she made the builders use wood from the Tree of Life for these columns as you see them here: red, white and green.'

They had listened for a long time and the tide was almost on the turn. The sea birds on the rock stacks screamed and quarrelled overhead and dived into the sea.

Dindrane said:

'Look again at that sword. It belonged to Solomon's father, King David. No more marvellous sword was ever forged, and the one who wields it will never be overcome in battle.

'Solomon's wife offered to produce a belt for the scabbard. She meant to have a fine leather one made, with studs of gold and silver; but for some reason or other she could never find a leather-worker to make it as she wanted. She lost heart, so in the end she made the tawdry belt of rope and metal that you see before you. "Some other woman will make a better belt one day," she said, "so let it be." She did not realise that she was foretelling what would happen to us this very day.

'When the ship was ready for launching Solomon was asleep nearby, and that night he had a vision of hands writing on the ship's side. When he awoke he found words painted on the ship, and those words were the ones you have all just read. Solomon was afraid to go on board, and while he stood hesitating, the ship glided away of her own accord; and since then she has travelled over all the oceans of the world. Now she has sailed to us.'

A Kind of Knowledge

They eyed the ship as though she might vanish from their sight. She was a ship of miracles.

Dindrane said 'The only one who may draw this sword on the bed is Galahad. It was forged for him, and the ship was built for him.'

Despite what she said, Galahad was hesitant, fearful that he might be tempting providence. Dindrane reassured him and he then drew out the sword; it fitted happily in his hand.

At this Parcival said 'This is all very well, but what about the new sword-belt we need? Who was the woman who was going to make one? What happened to her? Did she ever manage to replace this poor thing with something suitable?'

'How can we know?' said Bors. 'She must have died years ago. Do you expect her to appear to us in the middle of the ocean?'

As they were speaking impatiently, Dindrane brought her wooden box, which she opened and placed in Galahad's hands. Inside it lay a gleaming golden belt with two buckles of red gold, and thongs to affix it to a scabbard. At first he thought the belt was made of actual gold, then he realised that the metal threads were finely interwoven with Dindrane's own hair, the two shades of bright gold and honey gold creating the finest sword-belt he had ever seen. He handed the box back to Dindrane and removed the sword-belt he was wearing. Then she took the sword and the scabbard from the bed and buckling the belt around his waist, she attached the sword and its rose-red scabbard. She seemed filled with a secret joy as she turned to Bors and her brother, saying:

'Now I have done what I prayed to do; and if I should lose my life on this quest, it will be a price worth paying.'

For in her spirit she knew how the quest would end for herself and for them all.

Bors looked at her with affection. 'You will be safe with us' he said. 'We are all one company. No one will take your life.'

Galahad put his hand on the scabbard, saying solemnly 'Dindrane, you have done so much for me that I swear now to defend you in every danger, so long as I am free and within reach of you.'

Parcival, not to be outdone, took her by the hand and said 'We could not have a better guide than you, Dindrane. If we ever find the Grail, it will be because of you.'

They were silent for a time, sobered by what they had seen and heard. Presently Dindrane broke the silence.

'Galahad, look hard at your new sword.' she said. 'I told you that it has great power, and so it has; and yet that sword has brought ruin and devastation on the whole land.'

'How can that be?' asked Galahad, dismayed.

'It was through your own great grandfather, King Pellam' she told him. 'Years ago, when he was hunting in one of his forests, he got lost. So he and his companion followed a track that led them to the sea, to this very spot, where they found this very ship we stand in.

'He read the warning and scorned it. He went in the ship and tried to draw the sword from the scabbard; and at that very moment he was cut down by a flying spear. To this day, he is maimed and crippled, and no one has been able to heal him. Men call him the Wounded King because all his strength has seeped away.'

'In the name of God, Dindrane!' Galahad cried in protest, but she was not to be interrupted.

'More than that happened' she said. 'Not only was your King Pellam wounded but all the land was wounded with him. Rivers are polluted; fields yield nearly nothing; cattle have few young; leaves wither on the trees, and the very soil is blighted. His kingdom is called the Waste Land because his pride has ruined it. The whole order of the world has been shaken by his arrogance.'

They were silent. They had all heard about the plight of the Wounded King.

'One day you will reach the Waste Land' she said to Galahad, 'and Castle Carbonek where the Grail is. There you will heal the Wounded King and renew the suffering earth. That is part of your quest.'

They returned into their own sturdy ship, and a fine breeze arose which drove them northward. They sailed for days, with no idea of their destination nor of their position either, since fog came down and they drifted for a long cold night and part of a day. They did not realise that they were sailing along the coast of Scotland, but as the fog lifted they could see sharp cliffs, white with bird-droppings and old nests; and here and there seals on one of the rocky ledges. At length the ship drew into a small harbour backed by cliffs. They could already hear the trumpets of the watchmen, warning of the approach of strangers.

As they stepped on to the quay, a man ran towards them. 'Take my advice' he said. 'For your own sakes, go no further. Get back into your ship and sail elsewhere.'

Bors face took on a hard, suspicious look. 'Why should we?' he said.

'I'll tell you' the man replied. 'This is the kingdom of Galloway, and no strangers have ever entered it and lived to go home again. This is wild country, full of strange creatures and every sort of danger. Take my advice; I am speaking as a friend.'

'We are knights of King Arthur' Parcival said.

'Then you are in even more danger, for Arthur is the enemy of our king.'

They considered this seriously, and Galahad said 'We have not come all this way to give up now.'

The others all agreed. Then the man on the quay left them. With Dindrane in their midst, they made their way in a group up the narrow street, the three men holding swords in their hands.

Suddenly six mounted men appeared who rode swiftly towards them. Bors reacted first. He struck one rider with his sword so that the man fell sideways from the blow. Bors dragged him off the horse and took it for himself. Thus mounted, he drove furiously against a second knight whose horse reared and fell backwards, stunning its rider. Immediately Galahad seized this horse for himself, and he and Bors turned on the remaining riders and felled two more of them, at which the rest fled. Parcival had stayed with Dindrane, since she was unarmed; but now thanks to Bors and Galahad they were a mounted group again.

Free of the harbour town, they rode across a stone bridge and into hilly country covered with bracken and, here and there, rowan trees growing. No one disturbed them and they rode companionably. The hilly countryside grew more level and wooded. Gradually it became thick oak forest. At length they came to a great clearing that ran on until it was cut through by a swift river. A square castle and a tower stood in the clearing. They thought they would ride past unnoticed, but the watchman in the tower saw them and sounded his warning. In a short space of time they found themselves surrounded by a group of armed men, one of whom took Dindrane's horse by its bridle and made as if to lead it away. Parcival surged forward to protect her.

'Is this lady a king's daughter?' asked the man.

'Certainly she is' said Parcival. 'Take your hand away. She is the daughter of King Pellinore and Queen Ashfleur. She is my sister.'

The man was unmoved and said 'Then she must comply with the custom of this castle.'

He turned to the three knights and said 'The lady whose men we are has a deadly sickness. We know from doctors that she can only be cured by blood taken from a certain king's daughter. Every woman who comes this way, so long as she is a king's daughter, must give her blood so that possibly our lady will be healed.'

The three knights protested vehemently.

'What has your lady to do with us?' said Bors. 'This is a problem for you, not us.'

'She might die if she does this' said Galahad. 'What happened to all the others you have wounded for the sake of your sick lady?

'You will never put my sister's life in danger' said Parcival furiously. 'Let us pass. We have nothing to do with you.'

The man who held Dindrane's horse spoke to Bors as the eldest of the three. He said:

'We are twenty men. We can bring out fifty more, and you three cannot possibly overcome us if we fight. Be reasonable men. Spend the night here in this castle and let us explain our problem to you. I guarantee your safety, and a truce until tomorrow.'

The three knights argued and disagreed among themselves, but presently Dindrane urged them to accept the truce.

Unwillingly they obeyed her and let themselves be led into the castle, where they were now received with friendliness and expectation. Once again they heard the story of the lady whose only hope of healing was from the blood of another woman.

'She has suffered so much' said one of the knights, 'and now it is for you to decide what you will do.'

Dindrane spoke privately to the three, and asked their advice.

'It seems that it lies with me whether she is healed or not' she said.

They were all opposed to her cooperating.

'You may well die if you do so' Galahad told her, but Dindrane silenced him:

'If we refuse' she said, 'you will have to fight these men tomorrow and lives will certainly be lost, yours or theirs, and nothing will be gained. Whereas if I agree, the woman may be healed; and should I die, it is only one life that is lost.'

That night Parcival did not sleep because his thoughts were all of Dindrane. He spent hours wandering on the castle battlements, despite the cold of the night; and his apprehensions increased around midnight when clouds appeared in the sky, sending out vibrating rays of light – red, blue, white, green. Suddenly they vanished; to him they seemed a symbol of death.

Next morning the lady of the castle came to see Dindrane. She was young, not much older than Dindrane herself but gaunt and ravaged with disease. She told Dindrane how the sickness had encroached upon her for the last five years and she begged Dindrane for help. 'Perhaps after all this time, it is your blood that will heal me.'

They all sat in silence, their eyes fixed on Dindrane. At length she stood up and took the sick woman by the hand.

'Bring a knife' she said, and she folded her sleeve back to the shoulder. The castle physician had a knife at hand, small, sharp as a razor, and he cut deep into her vein. His assistant held a silver bowl for the blood, which soon overflowed the bowl onto the rushes on the floor. Despite the efforts of the physicians it went on flowing so that Dindrane grew faint and fell back onto a bench.

Parcival tried to staunch her blood but it was impossible. Then Dindrane spoke to the sick woman who was standing close by.

'Pray for me' she said. 'My life is draining away.'

After this she became senseless for a time, and then seemed to revive. She turned to the three companions who were in tears, and said:

'I beg you, do not bury me in this place. Let them build a ship for me and put me in it, and let it sail wherever the sea will take me.'

She said goodbye to them as they knelt beside her.

'Do not be sad' she told them. 'I am only going ahead of you, and we shall meet again. Now your quest will take all of you far away from here to the city of Sarras in the East. But when you sail into the harbour there, you will find me waiting for you.'

They sent for a priest, and the hermit who came prayed with Dindrane. Then she spoke for the last time, saying:

'From now on, each of you must ride alone, as you did at the beginning.'

The castle carpenters built a ship for Dindrane and they made it like the old northern ships that used to sail these seas. It was long and narrow, the planking tapered to form upward curving stem and stern pieces carved in the shape of sea birds. The ship had a single mast and one square sail.

The physicians embalmed Dindrane's body and wrapped her in linen from head to foot. Then her three companions laid her body in the forepart of the ship, spreading leather coverings as a protection. Beneath the cushion on which her head rested Parcival put a piece of parchment on which he had written the story of her journey with them, and who she was.

After that, all the people of the castle assembled with the knights to watch the ship set adrift on the river. Among them was the lady of the castle, now healed and rejoicing with her family. So it was a time both of gladness and grieving. Many of the onlookers stood sorrowfully with the three knights, and as the ship was carried away they said to one another 'Who was this woman who was ready to give her life for a stranger?'

A Kind of Travelling

CHAPTER 7

The Ship from the North

Lancelot rides for miles along the bank of an unknown river. One evening, as thick darkness falls, a ship glides into the river bank and a voice tells him to go on board. Next day he discovers that this is Dindrane's funeral ship. He reads her history which Parcival had written and placed beside her hand. Thus he learned what has happened to Bors, Parcival and Galahad.

Sailing on towards the sea with Dindrane's body, the ship enters a deserted harbour. Here to his amazement Lancelot finds Galahad. Father and son remain together for weeks, then Galahad goes on his way and the ship sails westwards, carrying Lancelot towards the Grail castle.

When Lancelot looked at his horse Traveller lying dead beside the river, it seemed yet another sign that his skill and strength had both dwindled away. In deep gloom he settled down to sleep.

When he awoke, it was barely dawn and white mist hung over the river. He noticed that further down it divided into two branches, and as he wondered which he should follow, a voice said to him:

'Lancelot, take your armour. Follow the left branch of the river and when you see a ship, go on board.'

He did as he was directed and made his way along the bank. On the far side were high rocky hills but on his side the slopes were lower, covered with gorse and bracken. The river gradually grew smoother and slower. He could see no sign of any ship though he looked back often enough.

He met a man cutting furze, and asked him what river this was.

'Well,' he answered, 'men say it comes from the far North, so we call it the North River. Sometimes in winter it brings pieces of ice with it, and so we also call it the Winter River; and it may have other names as well.'

'Do many ships sail on this river?'

'No, I have never seen one.'

Lancelot went on for some miles, and presently he arrived at a collection of half-ruined buildings and the remains of a mill. Still no ship appeared so he spent the night in the shelter of the buildings. Next day, seeing a narrow track that led inland, he decided to follow it.

By evening he was footsore and sweating, so he was greatly heartened to find himself coming into a village. It was quite a busy place with a market cross, a good stone church, and a hospice for blind men. Fortunately for him, a pilgrim's road passed through the village, and a hostel had been set up where sick pilgrims could rest, get food, wash themselves, or get their hair cut; or even consult the priest who was in charge.

He was only too glad to rest there among a group of noisy, garrulous pilgrims on their way home. The hospice was a cheerful place, too, because the pilgrims were given to singing; and their musicians entertained the company with bagpipes and fiddles all through the meal.

Two men who clearly did not belong to the pilgrim group gravitated towards Lancelot when it became known that he had no horse and could effectively go no further. These two were metal workers who travelled from place to place, making crucifixes and chalices, caskets for relics and clasps for books; to say nothing of the silver gilt studs and badges so necessary for decorating horses' harness and trappings. They knew all the horse copers in the area, and offered to act on his behalf. They came back with a dark bay gelding with poor, second hand trappings. He paid the quite large amount they asked for it. 'This would have kept me for a year' he said angrily to himself, and saw in his mind's eye his dead horse Traveller lying on the river-bank, still wearing his splendid tack with silver and gold rosettes brightening the leather. Nevertheless he was highly relieved to have a horse, any horse, rather than have to walk.

Soon the country grew more wooded, and he spent the next few days on a good green track through an oak forest. As he rode he could hear great shoutings and the blare of trumpets. He had come upon a tournament. In front of the square stone castle in the clearing, a mock battle was at its height: two groups of mounted men fighting with swords. Some of them were obviously wounded, and a few lay motionless on the grass. As the fortunes of war changed so the spectators, men and women, cheered on their men.

Lancelot had seen many a tourney, and he stood and watched. Soon it became obvious to him that the knights of the castle, a grim little army in black armour, were getting the worst of the encounter, being constantly divided and beaten back by their opponents. Lancelot admired the energy of these riders in their white armour, white pennants on their lances; men who would surely be declared the victors at the end of the day. Yet he felt for the black riders, wanted them to win, so he rode into their ranks where he set to with the utmost ferocity. But no matter how hard he fought, the white riders did not fall back. On the contrary, some of them made him their target and pressed upon him until he could barely hold his sword, and he felt he might fall from the saddle in sheer exhaustion.

A group of them cut him off from the main body, surrounded him and made him prisoner. Then they led him into another part of the forest, far away from the tourney. Here they released him, only saying to him as they left him:

'Never go back to those men again. Have nothing to do with those black knights.'

He did not understand. Until that day he had never been taken prisoner in a tournament, had never been beaten in a joust. He was full of chagrin, deeply disturbed.

'Look at me now' he said within himself. 'My God, I am ashamed that this should happen to me. I must be even more sinful than I thought.'

He rode on unhappily, until he was distracted by a tiny church built at the very edge of the track. He drew rein and studied it.

Built against the church wall he saw a lean-to with a little window, and he guessed that some recluse or anchoress must live there. Indeed he heard her greeting, asking his name and where he had come from.

He tied up his horse and went to the window. The anchoress was very old and bent, and she listened without moving as he told her about the strange happening at the tournament. He hoped she could explain it to him, but she was silent for so long that he thought she had forgotten he was there. Finally she spoke, and as she did so his dismay increased.

'Lancelot' she said, 'in the past you were the best knight of all, but that was when you searched for fame and power and money. Today your search is for the things of God, in so far as men and women can grasp them; and in this search many men are as good as you, and some far better.'

'My fortunes have changed' he said. 'I know I am not the man I was. My mind is divided. I am drawn in different ways. Things happen and I don't know what they mean.'

She said 'I can tell you what that tournament means. Two sorts of knights were fighting there, just as two sorts of knights are on this quest of yours. In the white riders you must see loyal single-minded seekers, whereas the black riders stand for knights who are divided men, self-seeking and disloyal. You joined those men whose hearts are as black as their armour because you know in your heart that you belong with them.'

She was silent again, looking at him with a certain satisfaction. Then she said:

'The white riders rescued you. They forced you out of that evil company. That was to show you that you must keep away from all their wiles; to remind you that so long as your heart is with the black knights you will never find what you are looking for.'

He knew that what she said was true, and bowed his head.

The old anchoress seemed sorry for him. She called her servant, a woman nearly as old as herself, and sent her to the priest's house. To Lancelot she said: 'I am concerned for you, for you are going to find yourself in strange territory before long. Have you had any food today?'

'No' he told her. 'I have barely eaten yesterday either'

'I knew it, I knew it' she said. 'So you shall share with me.'

Presently the servant brought him a wooden spoon and a wooden bowl full of leek porridge. Lancelot settled himself on the bench under the window, and when he had eaten he said goodbye to the old anchoress and thanked her.

'God bless you' she said. 'I believe he will make you a good knight.' Then she closed the black curtains and shut the window.

Lancelot's path had led him through bracken and over the crest of a hillock, and thence into a scrubby oak wood in which he could see wisps of smoke rising from among the trees. Soon he found himself by a poor chapel, and adjoining it a decrepit wooden hovel thatched with decaying rushes. Nearby, the ashes of a fire still smouldered. A priest ran out of the chapel crying 'Thank God! You have come at a good moment. Come with me. God keep you, sir, and tell me what to do.'

Lancelot followed him into the dark chapel. Lying on the earthen floor was the body of an old bearded man, bareheaded, barefooted. The body was dressed in a linen shirt, new, embroidered. It struck a strange note in the midst of the church's poverty and dilapidation.

'That linen shirt!' cried the priest. 'How did he get such a thing? This man has been a White monk for sixty years. He has lived in those woods for twenty and I knew him well. Everyone knew him. People came to him from all over these parts. I came today to speak to him and this is what I found.'

He paused and they both stared at the dead man and his shirt.

'I have great anxiety for him' said the priest. 'He was a good man and I loved him.. But he was a monk, and luxury is utterly forbidden him. So how did he come by that linen shirt? Surely he had not broken his vow to live in poverty? Surely he has not deceived us.'

He went on in this vein for some time, full of grief and worry. At last he seemed to make up his mind. He said to Lancelot decisively:

'Wait here. I will try to find out what has happened. I believe that demons are involved in this.'

He rummaged behind the little wooden altar in the dismal chapel and fetched a stole, a candle and a prayer book. He put the stole round his neck, gave Lancelot the unlighted candle and led him outside the church.

'I shall make these spirits tell the truth' he said, and began to read in a loud voice. As the priest prayed, Lancelot felt a chill of fear rise in him, for the earth by his feet began to writhe and to split, while a terrifying black shape was extruded from the fissure.

'Why have you called me up from the darkness?' it demanded. 'What do you want of me?'

Lancelot noticed that the priest showed no fear. Instead he said in a commanding voice:

'Tell me the truth. Is this man here saved, or is he lost?'

The demon answered in a grudging voice: 'He is not lost. He is saved.'

'Then why does he wear the linen shirt which no monk would be allowed to touch? And how did he meet his death? Tell me the truth.'

The demon said 'This monk of yours was once a great lord, and his family still lives in these parts. His nephew was attacked by the Earl of the Valley who was their enemy. The nephew came here for help so the monk you see here left his hermitage and went to fight for him. In the end a truce was made; but later the Earl of the Valley broke it and sent two men to take revenge.

The Ship from the North

'They attacked the old monk with swords but your God protected him. This enraged the knights so they lit a fire to burn him alive. Then the monk said "If I die, it will be by God's will, not by yours. This fire will not burn me; and if I wore the finest shirt in the world, the flames would never touch it." They laughed at this and mocked him, but one took off his own shirt and put it on the monk. Then they threw him into the fire, and the flames burned all day and night. The monk died but there is no mark of burning on him. Now that is the truth, so let me go.'

The clouds darkened, a sudden wind arose, the tree branches swung wildly, enveloping Lancelot and the priest in a wild flurry of autumn leaves. In the darkness Lancelot saw the demon rushing away, and as it went the ground was charred by its footprints.

Next day Lancelot and the priest buried the monk outside the chapel, and the priest blessed the grave, saying "This man was a true servant of God; and God has worked a miracle for him, as you yourself have seen.'

He was happy and relieved, and he invited Lancelot to stay that night with him, though there was little in the way of comfort in the tumble-down house where the dead man had lived.

'Sir,' he said, 'I believe that you are Sir Lancelot, the knight from Avalon.'

'I am' he said.

'Then what are you doing in these parts?'

'I am one of the knights searching for the Grail. I have been on this quest for well over a year. Sometimes I think I have no hope of finding it.'

'You may be right' the priest said. 'In the past, the fire of God's spirit burned in you; but no longer. Today your love and loyalty have changed. For you love Queen Guinevere, and you both betray the king.'

Lancelot was pierced by these words. He was wholly confused, thinking of his promise to avoid the Queen's company and then thinking of the old priest in the fire, a man who had been constant to God all his life, and whom God had vindicated in his death. He told this to the priest.

He answered 'You must know that it is the same for you as for that holy man we have just buried. He could never have reached his goal if God's mercy and goodness had not drawn him. Nor will you.'

'What must I do, then?'

'Open your eyes to all that God sends you' he said. 'God is directing your path through all that happens to you. So far, you have been blind to much of it.'

Lancelot said goodbye and rode back towards the North River, which gradually grew wider. While there was still some daylight left, he saw a ship sailing down the river; a long narrow ship with a single mast and a square sail. The prow was high, shaped like the head of a wild swan.

He slid off his horse and waited hopefully while the ship glided into the river bank. It was now too dark to see much but he turned his horse loose and went on board, stowing his sword and shield beside him. The ship moved with the flow of the river. He sat in the darkness, and now his spirits rose and he felt a happiness he had never felt since starting on the quest.

'Oh God' he said, 'you are beginning to show me where I must go. Keep me on your path, for Jesus' sake.'

When he awoke, the sun was shining. To his amazement he found that he was not alone. In the fore part of the ship lay the swathed body of a woman, her head resting on a sheet of parchment. Lancelot was astounded and totally taken aback, and sat there wondering who the woman could be and why God had let the two of them meet in this strange way.

Then he was inspired to read the parchment, and his astonishment increased as he learned that his companion was Parcival's sister.

'Dindrane led Galahad to the sea coast, where they met Bors and me. She joined us on our quest and sailed to Scotland with us. There she gave her life to save a sick woman. The people of that kingdom built this ship for her, and we set it on the river as she asked us. She says the sea will take this ship to some far city where all of us will meet again.'

As he read this, Lancelot's joy increased immeasurably for now he knew that Galahad, Parcival and Bors were travelling together. He put back the parchment, thanking God for this encounter and praying that he might meet his son.

The North River flowed into the sea, and Dindrane's ship rode easily over the small waves. Lancelot could see a number of grassy islets with never a tree on any of them. One in particular caught his eye for it was perfectly round in shape.

He wondered who lived in such a place and, as if in response, the ship took them to its sandy beach where a man was working energetically, stacking up great heaps of seaweed. He waved to Lancelot and shouted: 'What brings you here?'

'God's providence' said Lancelot. 'I have no idea where we are, nor where we are going. What is this island?'

'You would call it Grass Island' the man said, 'but we call it Mouse Island.'

'It's not like any mouse I ever saw' said Lancelot. 'Who lives here?'

The man laughed and stuck his wooden fork into the sand.

'Monks and laymen live here' he said, 'and cormorants and shags and every sort of sea-bird; and colonies of mice as well. We work the land and we fish; we pray, we try to live in peace together as the Lord Jesus commanded. But if we fail and fight among ourselves, he gives us a quick reminder; the mice become such a plague that no one has any peace, day or night. Then as soon as we are reconciled again, they vanish. So God sends them as brothers and sisters to teach us.'

He waded out into the water to the ship. When he saw the body of Dindrane, he was struck with astonishment and stood staring at her.

'What sort of ship is this' he cried, 'with a dead body on board!'

The Ship from the North

He was so bewildered that Lancelot told him about Dindrane's death, her wish to be set adrift on the water, and their strange meeting. When he learned that the man could read, he gave him the parchment. The man read it carefully.

'What a miracle!' he said. 'God has blessed you, letting you meet with such a woman. She will see that you reach the right harbour.'

He waded back to the beach and the seaweed, and waved goodbye.

'God go with you, servant of God!' he shouted. 'And when you meet your son Galahad, ask him to pray for me.'

After this, Lancelot and Dindrane sailed together for many days. There was little food on the ship but Lancelot's prayer gave him strength, as the sight of the Grail had strengthened them all in Camelot. He kept on recalling the man's parting words. 'Servant of God. He called me Servant of God' he thought, and his heart rose with expectation.

It was late autumn now, the time of rough weather. Yet though the days grew shorter and the sun less constant, still the breeze remained moderate and the surface of the sea showed no more than the movement of small waves just crested with foam.

They sailed from one island to another, sometimes finding themselves amid fishing boats; and sometimes Dindrane's ship took them among stacks of rock where sea birds screamed in alarm at their approach. One day the ship took herself right inside a deserted harbour where she came to rest against a half-rotted jetty of wooden planks. A track led uphill from the harbour, half hidden by overhanging trees.

Lancelot walked to and fro across the harbour, happy to have some respite from the sea, and as he walked he heard a horse coming down the track. A strange knight slowly rode towards him and dismounted. Lancelot did not recognise him. He stood warily taking his measure, because the rider was armed, while he had left his sword in the boat. The stranger came close, took off his chain-mail cap, held out his hands to him, and smiled.

'I am Galahad' he said. 'You were my beginning in this world.'

Then they fell on each other, kissing each other, laughing and weeping, filled with the greatest astonishment and joy.

'I am going to sail with you from now on' said Galahad, and he went on board the ship. When he saw Dindrane, he said 'This is the woman I honour most in all the world.'

'Tell me about your quest!' cried Lancelot. 'Tell me about Parcival and Bors; and where you have all travelled.'

So Galahad told him everything he could remember.

'It is nothing less than a miracle' said Lancelot. 'Never in my life have I heard of such things. It must be God who sent them.'

Then presently he said 'But what of Parcival's sister, Dindrane? Who has ever heard of her? Where did she get such wisdom to tell you all those things and to lead you as she did?'

Galahad said 'It must have been the inspiration of God's spirit.'

Lancelot and Galahad sailed with Dindrane for many weeks. This time they sailed far out into the ocean and for days they saw no land at all. Sometimes they drifted in fog, quite blind and full of fear that they might be approaching the place where sky and sea meet at the world's edge. When there was no fog, they would look with longing at the warning beacons lighted on distant rocks. During these weeks they used the time to speak of their hope that the Grail might show itself to them. In this way they gave strength to each other, though Galahad gave rather than received.

One day Galahad said 'Before long we shall come to land again.'

Soon after he spoke, a breeze arose which drove them to a small bay backed by high hillocks of grass. As they sailed in, they could see a knight riding through the dunes towards them. He rode a bay charger, and he was leading an ash grey horse. His voice came clearly over the water to them.

'Galahad!' he called. 'The time has come to leave Dindrane's ship. You have had long enough with your father. Now you must go on as providence will lead you. Take this horse and go into the forest.'

Then Galahad went to Lancelot and kissed him, saying 'I think we shall not meet again in this life.'

'Then pray for me' said Lancelot.

So they parted. Galahad took the grey horse and rode alone over the dunes and into forest, and soon he was lost among the trees.

Now a stronger wind began to blow, carrying Lancelot westward. Dindrane's ship sailed on as purposefully as though she had a navigator, making her way past high cliffs until she came to the wildest coasts of Wales. On top of the steepest cliff Lancelot could see a castle with four towers. Opening towards the sea, in the castle wall was a postern gate and a path cut in the rock that led down to the rocky beach. It was evening, almost dark, but the moon was full. As he looked at the castle, he heard a voice which seemed like the sea itself speaking to him:

'Lancelot,' it said, 'leave the ship. Dindrane has not ended her journey, but you have. Go up into the castle, and you will find something of what you long for.'

He took his sword and helmet, slung his shield round his neck and climbed up the path which was sometimes no more than steps cut into the stone. When he entered the castle, he had no idea that this was Carbonek where the Grail had rested since the days of Joseph of Arimathea.

Nothing seemed familiar to him as he went from room to room, finding no one. Yet he had been here before. Twenty years earlier he had first met Elaine, Galahad's mother in Carbonek. It was the birthplace of Galahad, the home of Elaine's father King Pelles, the castle of the old wounded King Pellam who had lain there for years and years, never finding healing.

The Ship from the North

All this bore out what people said of Castle Carbonek: that sometimes it became invisible, sometimes it changed its shape, while those who happened to come across it lost all memory of what they had seen. So Lancelot felt like a stranger, meeting no one as he climbed one stone stairway after another.

Finally he paused, for he heard the sound of singing. He followed the voices and came to a closed door. No matter how he tried, he could not open it. Meanwhile the voices sang:

'Holy, holy, holy Lord God Almighty. Who was, who is, and who is to come.'

Now Lancelot became convinced that the Grail vessel was in that room. He knelt and prayed with the greatest longing of his life, saying: 'Lord Jesus Christ, if I have ever done anything to please you, forget my sins and show me the Grail.'

The door opened of its own accord, revealing a room radiant with candlelight, a priest standing before a silver table, and on the table a vessel hidden under a silken covering. He recognised it at once and made to approach. At this, a warning voice said:

"Do not enter. This is not for you.'

Deeply disappointed, he stood and watched. He wondered if this was a vision, for when the priest turned round to raise the Eucharist bread in his hands, it seemed that the bread took on a human shape. At this Lancelot forgot the warning, and took two steps towards the altar. A terrible sheet of fire swept over him and he fell down, his sight gone, his hearing gone. He lay like a dead man.

For three weeks he neither moved nor spoke. Each day the castle doctor visited him, felt his pulse, raised his eyelids.

'He is certainly dead' said some of the visitors, but others disagreed.

"No, he is only asleep. He is in a trance and he will come out of it.'

The doctor remained non-committal while they argued.

On the twentieth day, Lancelot opened his eyes again. A dozen astonished faces stared at him.

'What happened to you?' people asked him.

'Where did your spirit go when you were senseless?'

'Tell us what you saw. Have you been with the dead?'

He could not reply. He had to grope for words; he was deeply moved.

At length he groaned and said 'I wish I had not come back'

'Tell us what you saw!' they cried again. 'Did you see angels then?'

'I have no words to describe what I saw' he said, 'but I know I would have seen much more had I been a truer man.'

He was silent then and refused to answer any more questions, much to their disappointment.

After a time he asked where he was, for he had no memory of his climb into the castle, nor his entry into the chapel.

'In Carbonek, the Grail Castle' they told him.

Then Lancelot remembered Elaine, and his first meeting with her and her father King Pelles, and her grandfather, the old wounded King Pellam. He got up from his bed and went to greet Pelles, who embraced him warmly, saying:

'Now I recognise you, Lancelot. You have come back to us.'

All the people in Carbonek who had known Lancelot before, now recognised him; because after his vision his face was exactly as they had known it twenty years before.

'Not all our news is joyful' said Pelles, and he told Lancelot that Elaine had been dead for more than ten years. This saddened Lancelot and he said: 'I honour her memory. She was young and beautiful, and she was the mother of the best knight of us all.'

When the doctor considered that Lancelot was fully healed, King Pelles made a great feast in his honour, sending invitations far and wide. They hung great painted cloths against the walls, and set up candles by the score. The place was packed with guests, with musicians, storytellers, singers and jugglers to entertain the company.

When the noisy feasting was at its height, a wandering knight rode into the courtyard, up to the very door of the hall and demanded admittance.

'Open up!' he shouted, beating the iron ring against the door. Servants were sent to dismiss him, but he was not to be silenced. Finally Pelles himself went to a window and spoke to him.

'This is no place for you' he said. 'Who are you? You are certainly no loyal knight on the quest, or you would never force your way into the castle of the Grail. You are some renegade and faithless man. Go somewhere else.'

The knight was furious and refused to leave.

'Then tell me who you are' said Pelles.

'My name is Hector of the Sea' he said angrily. 'My brother is Lancelot of the Lake.'

At this the king was greatly taken aback, and said:

'Why, your brother is with us at this very moment.'

'Lancelot is here?' cried Hector in amazement.

'We are celebrating his return from death.'

Suddenly Hector's rage fell away, for he remembered the hermit saying to him: 'One day you will try to gain admittance to a king's castle and you will be rejected.'

'My God,' he said to himself, 'it has come true. That hermit who warned Gawain and me was a prophet when he explained our dreams.'

He turned away, and without a word rode back the way he had come, a disturbed and apprehensive man.

When Lancelot heard that King Pelles had turned away his brother, he was insulted and angry. No one could persuade him to remain at the feast, and he rode off in search of Hector. He thought he would find him easily, but although he enquired of everyone he met, it seemed that Hector had

The Ship from the North

become invisible. No one remembered seeing a knight with a blue surcoat and a blue shield painted with three white scallop shells.

Lancelot rode for miles, along the coast, beside lakes and over hills and moorland, all of it now in the grip of winter. At length he came to the River Usk and followed it to where Arthur was encamped at Caerleon.

Here he found an atmosphere of gloom which muted the welcome he received. All the talk was about knights who had been captured or killed; or who, like Gawain, had returned disheartened.

The King seemed to have lost much of his resolution. He listened wearily as Lancelot described his own quest and then, so far as he was able to, the journeys of Galahad, Parcival and Bors.

When he had finished, everyone was silent. Then Arthur said: 'Oh, if only they were all here. They should never have gone on that quest, three such good knights.'

At that moment Lancelot had a glimpse of the future, and he said to Arthur: 'Only one of them will come back. The others we shall never see again.'

A Kind of Travelling

CHAPTER 8

The Lonely Season

Loyal to Dindrane's last wishes, the three knights go on their separate paths, as they had in the beginning. During these solitary months Galahad learns that Lancelot has left Carbonek and is returning to King Arthur.

Parcival begins to search for his friends, following up every clue. Of Bors he can learn nothing at all but he gets news of Galahad from a local recluse who foretells that he and Galahad will soon find one another. Before long Parcival and Galahad meet up on a wild moorland, beside a group of standing stones. Some time afterwards they come across Bors as well. From now on Bors, Galahad and Parcival will always journey together.

As Dindrane's ship was carried away by the river and disappeared from sight, the sky grew dark and heavy, and soon thunder began to roll round the sky. The knights could not endure the thought of remaining in the place where Dindrane had died, so they spent the whole night in the castle chapel.

In the morning, when all was calm again, they were amazed to find that one tower of the castle had been totally destroyed by the storm. Great masses of stone lay scattered everywhere.

'It is a judgement' said Parcival.

A path led from the chapel towards a garden with tall hedges, closed in by a gate of interwoven hazel branches. They went into the garden which was peaceful, the green grass still sparkling with the rain; and here they found some sixty graves, all of them carved with women's names. Of these sixty women, twelve like Dindrane had been the daughters of kings.

The three men walked silently from name to name, and Galahad said:

'Where can Dindrane be now? She could better be in peace with all these women than left to the mercy of the sea.'

But Parcival did not agree.

'It was her wish to sail in that ship' he said fiercely. 'She said she is going ahead of us and that we'd all meet again. And I, for one, believe her. She will keep her promise.'

But now there was confusion and fear at the castle, as its people examined the devastation created by the falling of the tower. Bors urged the other two to prepare to leave. He ordered their horses to be brought to them, asked for bread for their journey; and when they had armed themselves and hung their shields round their necks, they took a quick farewell of the lady of the castle, now fully restored to her former strength and dignity.

They were on the point of resuming their journey when they heard a voice speaking to them. It said:

'You have been true friends as you travelled together so many miles. But now you must do as Dindrane asked of you. Each of you must go alone. You must make your own way as you did in the beginning.'

They were all disappointed and downcast at this. Their love and understanding of each other had been deepened by sharing the hardships, joys and dangers they had met on the journey.

The voice went on, as though sensing their distress:

'This is not a final parting. One day providence will bring you together again. You will find your way to the wounded king and the Waste Land, and to Carbonek where the Grail is.'

'God grant it will be soon' said Galahad.

But this was to be the beginning of a long period of separation and loneliness.

'Let's say goodbye' said Bors, and they took off their helmets and embraced. Then they all turned towards the great dark forest that lay ahead of them, a mile or so away; each of them considering what tracks and clearings and roads he might find within it.

Suddenly from the edge of the trees they heard shouting and appeals for help as a mounted knight appeared, closely pursued by two armed men. The knight was clearly wounded, his surcoat red with blood, and he was barely able to keep himself in the saddle.

'Help me, God!' he kept shouting, looking desperately for assistance.

The two pursuers spurred on their horses, shouting triumphantly.

'He is calling on God' said Galahad, moved with pity for the man. 'I will go and help him.'

But Bors put out his hand and stopped him, saying:

'I will do it, Galahad. I can cope with these two. Leave them to me.'

He mounted his horse and rode grimly after the men, and he soon disappeared into the forest.

'Now we are only two' said Galahad, 'and God knows when we shall see Bors again.'

Parcival was silent. He needed to ride with people he knew and could depend on; he was afraid.

Galahad rode steadily south. Once clear of the dark wood he rode over heaths and commons and forded rivers, and crossed over marshy lands, but he could find no trace of Carbonek. He came to the sea coast and cliffs and sandhills, but he found nothing to remind him of the Grail Castle.

Though he had been born there and had lived there as a child, Carbonek was unknown territory. All he knew was what everyone knew: that the place was inaccessible unless God showed the way. The castle was invisible, said some; it moved like the islands that moved in the sea; it was built on high cliffs on a grassy mound; in a deep valley; it was mostly ruined; it was a celestial city never touched by storm. What is more, people said, travellers who might come across it once would never be able to retrace their steps and find it again.

So Galahad rode for almost a year, never reaching his goal. He did, however, find traces of his companions though he never met them in person. Chance brought him back to the Benedictine monastery where he had left the wounded Melias in the first weeks of his quest.

The guestmaster recognised him, greeted him with many words of welcome and promised him the best bed in the pilgrims' quarters. When he had seen Galahad disarm and lay aside his sword and shield, he led him to his own office and seated him on a bench.

'I have news for you' he told him. 'Your friend Lancelot has been here, though it was months ago. He was searching for his brother Hector; he was concerned for his safety. He said that he'd looked for him all over the countryside but no one could tell him anything.'

'What happened to Hector?' Galahad asked. 'Was he wounded, then?'

'No. It seems that he received some great insult, and rode away because he couldn't challenge the man who gave it. When Lancelot heard about this he rode after him. He came here, thinking that Hector might have asked for shelter in this house.'

The monk could tell him nothing more, only that Lancelot had ridden off in great haste and anxiety.

Early next morning Galahad went into the abbey church for the office of Prime. As he went in, he saw a newly-made tomb and beside it golden candlesticks in which wax candles burned.

He looked closer at the stone effigy and was shocked to see the image of his friend Bademagus. On each side of his tomb three shields had been carved into the stone, each shield with a singlemasted ship; for Bademagus had ruled the Isles of the Sea.

Galahad knelt sorrowfully beside the tomb, wondering how this good man had died. Then his eye fell on the inscription carved above the shields:

PRAY FOR KING BADEMAGUS
WHO WAS SLAIN BY GAWAIN, NEPHEW OF KING ARTHUR

He was distressed beyond measure by these words, and immediately sought out the guest master to ask what he knew about this death.

'I cannot tell you much' he said. 'I believe there was some quarrel between them. Gawain is a violent man. He rode away and left the body of the Scots king to be buried in our church.'

Galahad asked himself what madness could have made Gawain attack a fellow knight, a sworn companion. Then he remembered the seven brothers whom Gawain had killed, all of them wounded men. He prepared to leave the abbey with a heavy heart, grieving for Bademagus and full of foreboding.

As he was about to mount his horse and ride away, some of the monks detained him.

'Sir' they said, 'will you help us? Come down into the crypt of our church with us.'

His mind was still on Gawain, and all he wanted was to ride away, but the monks urged him to stay. He slid off his horse and went with them down the stone staircase to a collection of flat stone slabs, each carved with the name of a man long dead. The crypt was full of flickering shadows because small blue flames were continually springing up from one of the tombs, falling back and reviving.

'What does this mean?' asked Galahad. 'Why are these flames burning?'

The monk said 'We don't know. We cannot put them out, though we've tried often enough. We believe that only one man can do so. Will you try?'

Galahad hesitated.

'If God allows it' he said. 'Take me to where the body lies.'

Then they took him below the crypt into a cave full of stone coffins, on one of which the same flames were burning. As they stood there they all heard a voice from the coffin which said:

'Galahad, give thanks to God. He has given you power to help the dead as well as the living. I have been here since Joseph of Arimathea and his family built God's church in Avalon. I once did Joseph a great injustice in my life, but now I know by your coming that God has forgiven me.'

As the dead man told his story, the flames on the stone coffin flickered and went out one by one. They stood in silence.

'Take off the cover' said Galahad.

He and the monks studied the dead man. He was wearing the strangest iron helmet they had ever seen. One hand rested over a great iron sword, and on the other hand he wore enamelled rings on three of his fingers. It was hard to believe that he had lain there since the days of Joseph of Arimathea.

When Galahad had taken away the sword, handing it to one of the monks, he took up the body and brought it into the church. Next day the monks buried it in a side chapel.

'What shall we carve on the stone?' the monks asked one another, 'for nobody knows who he was.'

They could not agree so they asked Galahad for his opinion.

He told them: 'Write: Peace to you, Christian man from the East.'

Then he took his horse and said goodbye.

★

Meanwhile Parcival was riding from one monastery to another, one castle to another, hoping to find Galahad. Sometimes he got news, and often it was useless news that sent him gallivanting all over the countryside,

His long journeys took him to manors and convents, little villages and hamlets, and now and then to partly-ruined towns built long ago by the Romans. One such town he visited was Caerleon which stood beside the River Usk, and here he was given hospitality by the Augustinian Canons who manned the church of St. Aaron, a holy man martyred many years before by the Romans.

It was here that Parcival began to remember the advice pressed on him by his mother before he left Wales to become a knight.

'Always worship God' she had told him. 'Remember to go into churches and minsters when you pass by, and pray for honour in this world and a good welcome in the next.'

So he took to praying in St. Aaron's church, and in the church of St. Julian which was the home of a large community of Benedictine nuns; and even in the little chapel on the bridge over the river. He did not pray as his mother had advised; his only prayer was that he might find Galahad and Bors again.

At length one of the canons showed him some of the other sights of Caerleon, including the school of astronomy where a hundred learned men studied the movements of the stars, so that they could forecast strange events like eclipses of the sun and moon; the coming of great storms and floods; the deaths of great men; the dates of falling stars and comets.

When Parcival rode away his mind was full of what he had seen and heard. It was dusk and the sky was full of stars overhead. He considered the magnitude of space, the hidden secrets of the stars and of the earth; and he wondered if the scholars could predict the day when the Grail would manifest itself again.

Meanwhile he prayed to St. Julian who, said the canons, was the patron of travellers and would surely bring his search to a good conclusion.

One day Parcival heard church bells ringing and he hastened towards the sound, for he believed that the sound of church bells kept men safe from evil spirits. He came into a fair-sized village where a wheel-headed stone cross stood in the churchyard. The manor house, the church and the farms were surrounded by fields of oats and barley which presently dwindled away into heathland and thin stands of birch and aspen trees.

After he had visited the church Parcival was greeted by a baldheaded man who asked him 'Sir, have you come to get the blessing of our anchorite?'

'Why, no' he said, 'I know nothing of any anchorite but I will happily ask his blessing.'

'Then you may have to wait' said the man, who was the priest's clerk, 'for many people, bishops and wise men come to see him. He has made our village known far and wide.'

Parcival handed over his horse to the clerk, who put it in the care of the priest's servant. Meanwhile he sat on a bench outside the stone cell that was built on to the church wall.

After some time a couple emerged, the woman weeping silently, the man grim-faced as they waited for their servant to bring their horses. The priest's clerk watched them ride away, then he approached Parcival, again sat down beside him and said in a satisfied tone of voice:

'Yes, we get every sort of pilgrim here. Our anchorite is a holy man. Everyone here will tell you the same. People say he can work miracles, and I know for a fact that he healed a blind boy once.'

'How long has he lived here?'

'Twenty years or more. Before that he was a scribe in a monastery and copied books all day long. He has books with him in his cell, and sometimes he carries on with his old work.'

He got up and said 'Wait here, and I will find out if he is willing to see you.'

Presently the clerk returned and led Parcival into a tiny room. It was empty, with a door leading into a second room, in the door of which a window had been cut. This was where the anchorite lived, and he usually gave his counsel from the inner room. But as Parcival came in, he opened the door and greeted him as though they were old friends and of the same age, whereas he could have been Parcival's grandfather.

'What is your name?'

'I am called Parcival the Welsh man.'

'Well, Parcival' he said, 'you can eat with me first.'

So they ate a loaf of rye bread and drank some water. Then the anchorite asked Parcival why he had come to these parts.

'I am one of the knights searching for the Grail' he told him. 'It must be two years since we set out. I was riding with old friends but some time ago we had to separate. Now I am anxious to find them again, but so far I've looked in vain.'

'Tell me about this quest' said the anchorite. 'I know that the Grail is a hidden treasure that will only show itself to those with undivided hearts.'

So Parcival told him everything he could remember, from Galahad's arrival at Camelot to Dindrane's death in Scotland and their subsequent parting.

The anchorite listened as though all this was familiar to him.

'About your sister' he said, 'I can promise that you will meet her again, though I cannot say where. Galahad, too, is waiting for you and you will find him by some ancient stones, but I don't know when it will be. Meanwhile you should make your way to the White monks' abbey where you saw the old king Mordrain. Once you are there you will be guided by what God sends you.'

Parcival was amazed. 'You can see into the future' he said.

'Not I' said the priest, 'I have only partial knowledge as God gives it to me. My knowledge is like the knowledge of the birds. You know what people say: the eagle knows where to find its food but not when; the raven knows when but not where.'

After this he stood up and took a book from a shelf above his head. He unwrapped the green cloth around it, opened it and laid it down in front of Parcival.

'I will help you' he said. 'I will give you a gift for your journey. I want you to learn part of this page while you are with me.' He pointed to the place and said softly 'These are the sacred names of God. You must never say them except in times of danger. And you must never tell them to anybody else.'

He whispered these names into Parcival's ear:

'Holiness, Power, Compassion, Immortality, Strength and Splendour.'

Parcival repeated them, and struggled to memorise them.

'God is all that' the anchorite said, 'and he is more, for these are only words and God is beyond any words we know. Still, these are wonderful names to use. Which do you think the best?'

Without hesitation, Parcival answered 'Strength is a good name; so is Splendour.'

'As for me' the hermit said, 'My first choice is Compassion; that is God's best name.'

★

While all this was happening, Galahad was riding south, passing through towns where the buildings amazed him with their size and grandeur, through sprawling villages clustered round their church. These were much more familiar to him. He rode for many weeks, finding shelter in monasteries or pilgrims' hostels, sometimes in the homes of foresters or ferrymen, occasionally with parish priests who could afford to be hospitable; for most of them were as poor and ill-housed as their people.

One day Galahad found himself back at the Cistercian abbey in the forest clearing, the place where he had last seen Bademagus, the monastery where he had received the white and red shield he carried.

The monks recognised him and greeted him as a friend. Galahad noticed that they had finished clearing the surrounding forest, that now they had started to divert part of the river to irrigate the fields, and to create a channel for a water-mill. He marvelled at the order and determination shown by this endless labour.

When the guest master had shown Galahad to a cold little room and watched him take off his shield and disarm himself, he pointed to the shield and said 'That was once the treasure of our house.'

'I know' said Galahad. 'Before it came to me, it was owned by King Mordrain; and they say it was given to him by Joseph of Arimathea.'

'No, by his son Josephus' said the monk. He added:

'Did you know that King Mordrain is in our abbey now, a living man?'

Galahad was struck dumb. 'No one can live so long' he said. 'It was hundreds of years ago.'

'Well' the monk said, 'he is wasted away and blind, it is true. He lives at the point where life and death meet in the same breath, but he says he won't die until he sees with his own eyes the knight who is to find the Grail.'

Next morning very early Galahad presented himself in the cold, dark church. One of the monks said the Mass prayers turned towards the stone altar, never adverting to the presence of the few men and women who stood behind the wrought-iron screen.

When Mass was over, the guestmaster lighted a taper and took Galahad into the chancel towards the wooden bed where Mordrain lay motionless. They could hear him praying:

'Lord Jesus, let the Grail knight come here, and let me see him clearly.'

Galahad went closer. 'God bless you, my father' he said.

The old man sat up and his sight returned. He raised his arms and said 'I see you, I know you, Galahad. I have waited four hundred years and more for you. Sit beside me.'

Galahad obeyed, and took the old man in his arms. He weighed no more than a bird, and his arms were like twigs on a tree.

'Galahad,' he said, 'you bring goodness with you. The warmth of the Holy Spirit is in you.' And he bent his old head to rest on Galahad's shoulder.

After a pause he said: 'Lord Jesus, there is nothing more I want now, except to go to you.'

They buried Mordrain in the abbey garden which was also the monks' graveyard, a grassy circle surrounded by earthen banks and a green hedge. They gave him the place of honour near the wooden cross. The abbot read the prayers for the dead, with monks, lay brothers and labourers standing silently, lighted candles in their hands.

Galahad remained in the abbey until one of the brothers had time to make a wooden cross and to carve these words on it:

MORDRAIN, KING OF SARRAS, SERVANT OF CHRIST

Then Galahad took his leave of the monks.

'I will ride towards the west' he said, 'and maybe my road will lead to Carbonek.'

He rode many miles over moorland studded with rocky outcrops. Here and there he came on ruined stone walls and the scars from ancient tin mines. The moors grew wilder and more desolate. He drew up his horse and looked around. He could see a circle of some twenty standing stones which men of an earlier age must have set up. Some stones had fallen against their neighbours; all of them had been shaped by rain and frost and the gales that raced across these moors. Beyond the circle stood a group of three taller stones, and Galahad wondered if they were some sort of marker for he noticed that they stood facing the east and the sunrise.

Here he dismounted, hobbled his horse, leaned against one of the stones and ate some bread. He fell asleep and did not wake up till long after daybreak.

And here, as the anchorite had foretold, Parcival caught up with him.

When they had recovered from their astonishment and delight, and told and retold their stories to each other, they thought of Bors. Neither had any news of him since he had left them after Dindrane's death.

'Did he rescue that man, do you think? said Parcival.

Galahad had no doubts. 'But God knows where he went after that.'

'How can we ever find him?' said Parcival. 'We need another miracle like our meeting when Dindrane brought you to the ship.'

They rode over the moors and, passing through a sheep and cattle fair, they found themselves on the drovers' road. Coming upon a pilgrims' hospice, they spent the next day there. It was almost the beginning of winter and the pilgrims looked pinched and cold, huddled near a meagre fire. Many of them were women, and here and there a child's voice could be heard.

Parcival asked where they had come from.

'From Winchester, from St. Swithin's shrine' said a woman.

'Who was St. Swithin?' he asked, being more familiar with the Welsh saints David, Samson and Illtyd; not forgetting the many holy men of Bardsey Island.

She was surprised at such ignorance.

'Why, he was born in these parts. Everybody knows that. He used to be buried in a village not far from here, but then the bishop took his body and put it in the cathedral in Winchester. That was a long time ago but now we have to go to Winchester to see his shrine; and now the cathedral gets all the pilgrims' offerings.'

One of the men joined in the conversation, saying 'St. Swithin never wanted to go to Winchester, either.'

'No, he didn't!' cried the woman indignantly. 'People saw him crying when they took his body there. Do you know what happened next? It rained for forty days solid when they put his relics in that shrine, poor man. That shows that heaven didn't agree with what the bishop did.'

'And today' said the second speaker, 'if it rains on St. Swithin's Day you can be sure you'll have rain for the next forty days.'

Next day pilgrims and knights went on their respective ways.

'Let's go North' said Galahad, 'and see what we find. Maybe God has put Bors on the same path.'

Their new road led them through flatter land cut through with ditches. Next day they followed the river until they came to a busy village.

A bearded man was standing on the bridge. He told Parcival and Galahad that he was responsible for the safety of the crossing, for keeping watch on the height and fierceness of the river. He was also a hermit, he said, and would give them shelter for the night.

He was as good as his word. The horses had straw and a bowl of barley, the men a pot of porridge and a bed of straw on the earth-floor of the shack.

They told him about their quest and he made no comment except to pray that God would guide them. When he asked where exactly they were making for, they were silent.

85

He said 'There are many abbeys and suchlike around here. You might get help from one of them. We've got White monks here and Black monks, and Cluniacs and Black Canons. I used to be a brother with the Black monks in Michelney. That's not so far away. It's built on an island in the middle of the marshes. They might give you advice.'

He paused and reflected.

'Or you might go to Witham' he said. 'That's not an abbey, it's a new sort of brotherhood. They're hermits but they have an abbot. Each one lives in a log cabin where he works, and digs his own garden. It seems that they only meet together on Sundays and saints' days.'

'I have never heard of such men' said Parcival. 'How can they be hermits if they have an abbot and meet together?'

'Are there any other groups like them? asked Galahad.

'There may be, in other places' said the bridge-keeper, 'but I don't know of any.'

Next day they left the river and set out on a track over flat marshy land. It was late in the year now, with cold winds and once even a flurry of snow. Following the directions of the bridge-keeper they came to a lake. White mist rose up from the water, half hiding the cluster of modest buildings on the banks.

They had arrived at the charterhouse of Witham. They remained there for three days of ceaseless rain. They were not housed in the log cabins they saw, each with its own garden, all set in a circle, but in a building that adjoined the church. The room had a hearth and some logs of wood, and they lit a fire gratefully.

Apart from the brother who brought them food once a day, they saw no one, heard nobody, spoke to nobody. These days were a new experience, a strange interlude in their journey. Every day seemed the same. The hermits prayed and worked inside their cabins, the rains fell, the swans moved silently over the lake, the brothers in the house got on with their work with never a word. Galahad and Parcival hardly exchanged a word either, so compelling was the silence.

On leaving, they asked the brother what had brought men to this place. He said 'Some folk cannot find God in the middle of the monks' common life with all its distractions. They come here to leave all that behind, to learn to know God, to have God alone as their goal. We live as solitaries, as monks once did in Egypt in the desert, but we come together with our brothers because the Lord commanded us to love one another.'

Galahad said 'You are like the Templar knights in Jerusalem. They are knights and they are also monks. You are hermits, yet you are also monks. You both show something new.'

'God is offering us many new things in these days' said the brother.

As they journeyed, the landscape changed and they had to make their way through a lonely forest; a silent world of beeches and fallen leaves where no one was riding, it seemed, except themselves. But when they emerged from the darkness of the trees, they both caught sight of a solitary knight riding ahead of them. There was something familiar about him and the way he rode, and Galahad cried 'Surely, that is Bors!'

They galloped towards him, immediately recognising his blue shield with its silver star. They were filled with joy and elation; they could hardly believe their good fortune. They rode no further that day but hobbled their horses, and settled themselves at the forest edge. Bors brought food from his saddle bag. The others had nothing to offer in this line, being more improvident and more sanguine than Bors; so they all feasted on his barley bannocks and some cheese.

Parcival was full of his visit to the anchorite and to the charterhouse, and of all the wonderful things he had heard in the school of astronomy. Galahad told them about his journey in the ship with Lancelot and Dindrane, and they all marvelled at such providential happenings.

'And what about you, Bors?' asked Galahad.

He said 'Well, I have no great things to tell you. In all this time, I have only slept ten nights in a house, on a bed. I have slept inside a sheep pound in the hill country and in foresters' empty lodges, and once in a hospital for old blind men. All the rest of the time, I was in the open, in woods or caves, or cattle shelters, in all sorts of outlandish places. I would never have survived if God had not sent help to me.'

They fell silent at last, spent by so much talking. They were a tired and shabby-looking group by now, their chain armour rusting, their helmets dented, their trappings torn and faded, and their horses as weary as themselves.

Then Parcival said 'Bors, did you find what we are looking for? We haven't.'

'No' said Bors, 'I haven't found it.'

'We don't know where to go, or what to do next.'

'Nor do I' said Bors, 'so God must show us.'

A Kind of Travelling

CHAPTER 9

The Meeting Place

Having failed in their quest so far, the three knights entrust themselves to providence, agreeing to take the first westward road they meet. This leads them to the Waste Land, where they find Carbonek, the Grail castle, and are welcomed by Galahad's grandfather, King Pelles.

At Carbonek their understanding of the Grail is raised to a new plane when they are shown the vessel openly, unveiled. Furthermore, they have a vision of Christ during Mass in which he sends them on a still further journey; they are to take the Grail and sail with it to Sarras, far to the east.

After their meeting at the forest edge Bors, Parcival and Galahad rode across a sweeping valley, all brown with furze bushes. A wide river flowed ahead of them, and beyond it they could see a church and a substantial cluster of buildings. As they drew nearer they heard singing and shouting, and saw a great assembly of people gathered round the church. All along the river bank and outside the churchyard walls women were frying pancakes and selling cider to the crowds.

Parcival paused to speak to one of them.

'What is happening?' he asked. 'What village is this?'

The woman turned a pancake out of the pan and poured another ladle of batter into the hot fat.

'This is the feast day of our village' she said.

Parcival was none the wiser. 'What feast day?'

'This, sir' she told him, 'is the feast of St. Eluned, our saint. She's buried here in the church. You can see her relics; they're in a silver shrine. People come from all over Wales to be healed by her.'

He looked around him at the churchyard, astonished to see men and women hand in hand dancing over the graves. They made a long human chain which constantly entered and re-entered the church, everyone singing at the top of their voices. To him it seemed a strange way to seek healing, especially as one or other dancer would collapse, only to be pushed aside until their senses returned.

'Do you know this saint, Parcival?' asked Bors. 'She's Welsh like you.'

'Not I' he said. 'The Snow Mountains are my home. Still, I did hear about a holy woman there called Winifred, and people are cured at her shrine, too.'

The woman overheard these words and said in hasty defence of their own holy woman 'That may be, but our Eluned was the daughter of a king. She had twenty-three sisters, all of them holy women, but she was the holiest of them all. Sir, go into the church and see if she doesn't help you in all your needs.'

They would have liked to follow her directions but the dancing of the crowd made any entrance impossible. They rode away deeply impressed, imagining the relics and their power to heal.

'She must be a saint of the old days' said Parcival, 'like Dyfrig or Brendan.'

There was no prospect of hospitality in St. Eluned's village on such a busy day, so they rode on and spent the night in a half-ruined stone barn. Next day they discussed how they might find the road that led to Carbonek where the Grail was.

'How much can you remember of Carbonek?' Parcival said. 'At least you have both been there.'

But the other two had little memory of it, save that it stood high above the sea on steep rocky cliffs.

Bors said 'When Lancelot vanished from Camelot years ago, Queen Guinevere sent some of us to bring him back, and we found him in Carbonek. I can only remember how often it was hidden by mist rising from the sea. I think, though, that it stands near a great expanse of moorland and forest. That is all I can tell you.'

'I remember nothing about it' said Galahad. 'I only know what people say.'

They would have gone on discussing Carbonek, but Bors put an end to it.

'Let providence direct us' he said, 'for we certainly shan't find it of our own accord. So I propose that we take the first road leading to the west and stay on it, come what may.'

They obeyed him, and as they rode through oak woods, the trees steadily diminished and became bent and stunted, shaped by years of salty winds; distorted, covered with moss and lichen. Fallen trunks were mouldering away, ferns growing from the broken bark.

After journeying for about a week, they all began to notice that the countryside was changing. There was no bird-song, no movement among the trees. It was unlike any other place they had encountered, and it chilled them with its atmosphere of half-life and decay. Thorns and thistles grew abundantly but the earth was dry and dusty, and the stream held no more than a trickle of water. Many trees had fallen and lay one against the other; and the upright trees were mostly skeletal, without a leaf on them.

Galahad felt as though no human voice had ever been heard in this diseased and ailing land. But he was wrong, for they came across a solitary man, a charcoal-burner, black with soot and smoke. He turned to them from the smouldering heap he was covering with the dried up earth.

'Friend,' said Galahad, 'what is this place?'

'Sir,' said the man, 'this is the Waste Land. You'll find no future here; it has all been ruined.'

The Meeting Place

'How long has it been like this?'
'Longer than anyone remembers.'
Bors asked: 'How far does this Waste Land stretch?'
'Sir' he said, 'none of us knows the length of it.'
They rode on in silence. Even the grass was no longer green but withered. It was almost a desert, and the small woodland creatures had long since died away.

But if they saw no other human beings, they themselves were seen. When the watchman on the tower of Carbonek blew his horn to indicate the coming of day, he saw three mounted men afar off riding towards the castle.

The news was quickly brought to King Pelles, and he and his knights were full of anticipation.

'No one has ridden through the Waste Land until now' they said. 'These three are surely the ones Merlin spoke about.'

King Pelles himself went down into the courtyard and welcomed the arrivals. Once their horses had been led away, he took them into the castle itself where they were all glad enough to be relieved of their armour and weapons, to wash the rust and grime from their faces, to put on long woollen robes and shoes of good Spanish leather.

King Pelles was a happy man, seeing Galahad his grandson again after fifteen years or more. And there were a number of people in the castle, Elaine's women in particular, who remembered him and went out of their way to welcome him with great affection.

One of King Pelles' men remembered the day when Bors had found Lancelot in Carbonek, and like Bors he was a veteran of many battles. He took Bors' hand in his and said:

'This is a good time for all of us. The spell that lies over this kingdom will be lifted through your coming. Galahad is going to restore the old king's health and unlock the waters which were dried up by the spell, so that the earth can flourish again.'

'We heard about that from Parcival's sister' Bors said. 'She told us about the sword that wounded King Pellam.'

'I am the same age as our King Pelles' said the knight, 'so I can just remember the land before the old king ruined it by his arrogance. It was like a paradise: rivers and streams that never failed; wells dug so that all travellers could refresh themselves; trees flowering and crops growing; all the people happy, and birds singing, too.'

Evening drew on and the sky, already heavy with clouds, grew quite black and a strong wind began to blow, rattling the wooden shutters at the windows, blowing drifts of smoke from the fire near which King Pelles and the whole company were gathered. As the wind rose to gale force they looked uneasily at one another. Then suddenly each one heard a voice which said:

'The good knights will soon come to the Lord's table; only they may remain here.'

At this the company withdrew, puzzled and apprehensive, leaving the three knights alone with King Pelles, his son Eleazer and a niece of his. The six of them sat in silence, wondering why these words had been spoken.

Presently they heard the sound of footsteps approaching as nine men fully armed tramped into the hall. They paused, set down their shields against the walls, took off their chain-mail helmets, withdrew their swords from their scabbards and placed them on a table. They went to Galahad, holding out their hands in greeting.

'We have travelled in great haste to be with you at this table' said one of them. 'We have come from distant places.'

'You are welcome' Galahad said.

Three of the men wore red surcoats, three wore green, the rest wore blue.

'Where have you come from?' he asked.

'Three of us are from Gaul' they told him, 'three are from Ireland, and three of us are Danish knights.'

As they were speaking, the door opened again. This time four young women entered carrying an ivory bed, one woman at each corner. After them came four knights, each with a burning candle in his hand. The wax of these candles was so pure that it burned brighter even than the magic candles Merlin had made years before in memory of all the kings who died in Arthur's wars.

When the knights had placed a candle at each corner of the bed, they and the women withdrew without a word.

An elderly man lay on the bed, covered with a purple woollen quilt, his head resting on a pillow that gave out the scent of rosemary. He looked pale and withered, totally bereft of energy.

Galahad looked hard at him. He had no memory of this old man.

Bors said within himself: 'So this is King Pellam, the Wounded King, the man who disobeyed God's warning in the ship; the man who brought suffering on himself and on the earth as well.'

Parcival remembered what Dindrane had told them about this man. 'He is Galahad's great grandfather' he said to himself.

King Pellam raised himself and called Galahad.

'Galahad! Thank God that you have come! I have been waiting for you all these years, but now I know that my pain will find relief; that you will heal me.'

The sound of the wind which had subsided now rose again to its former violence, and again a voice came from it saying:

'There are still some of you here who are not searching for the Grail. You must leave now.'

At this Pelles, his son and his niece withdrew. The old king fell back on his bed and lay still, and sometimes a groan came from him. When he heard this, Bors remembered the knight telling him that sometimes the Waste Land, too, cried out because of the suffering Pellam had brought upon it.

The Meeting Place

As they stood in silent expectation the twelve men were all granted the same mysterious vision. It seemed to them that they stood facing a silver table on which the Grail vessel stood, not hidden as it had been in Camelot but standing free now of its covering.

As they watched they became aware that a man was seated beside the table. He wore a bishop's robes, and a headband on which they read these words:

JOSEPHUS, FIRST BISHOP OF SARRAS.

This was beyond their comprehension. They knew that Josephus had been dead for hundreds of years. When he saw their bewilderment he smiled and said:
'Don't be afraid. I used to be an earthly man like all of you.'

While they were still wondering if this was a dream the door opened and they saw a file of angels, some with lighted candles, one holding a lance from which drops of blood fell into the silver bowl he held in his other hand. Once they had placed the candles and the lance on the table the angels vanished.

Then Josephus stood up, calling them to come close to the table. No one dared to move. They had all been present at many Masses before this, in abbeys and priories and in castle chapels, but it had always been as onlookers. This was the role they were used to so they hesitated when Josephus drew them into his own prayers and action. Josephus lifted the Grail vessel from the table, took the eucharistic host from it and raised it high, showing it to each knight in turn.

For all of them this was a totally new experience. They had never been shown the host before, had never been close enough to know what the priest did at Mass. So they looked on in wonder, and in some cases in real fear and dread.

Suddenly they realised that Josephus had vanished and that Jesus himself was standing beside the table. They knew who he was because his hands and feet showed the crucifixion wounds. He took the Grail vessel in his hands and said to them:

'You have gone on your quest with courage. You have never given up. So now I will let you see something of my secrets. In the past Arthur's knights were given food and strength from this vessel, but none of them ever saw it face to face as you do at this moment.'

As Jesus went towards them they realised that he intended to give them the eucharistic bread. They were utterly taken aback, full of fear, wondering if they were caught up in the texture of a dream. None of them had ever received the host before; they had never seen any other knight receive it. It was part of the priest's life but not theirs; their role was to be present. In any case they were unworthy, for who could ever fulfil the demands for abstinence and purity which the Church demanded from anyone who wanted to receive Communion?

Yet despite prohibitions and present terrors they all received the host he gave them in awe, in total silence and with a sober joy they had not known till then.

Jesus still stood there, the Grail vessel in his hand, and he spoke to Galahad:

'Do you know what I am holding?'

'No, Lord' he answered. 'Tell me what it is.'

'This is the dish I used at my last supper, when we ate the paschal lamb. I gave this dish to Joseph of Arimathea. He gave it to his son Josephus, and since then their sons and daughters throughout the years have guarded it for me. In the past, some of Arthur's knights and some of Joseph's family, too, were given food and strength from this vessel but none of them received what you have just received. None of them ever saw it face to face, as you have done.'

After a pause, he spoke again.

'One day you will see into the very depths of this vessel. That will be in the future, in the city of Sarras. It is your mission to take the Grail there. This very night it is to leave this place, because people here neither serve it nor honour it. Tomorrow you must ride to the sea where you will find Solomon's ship. Take Bors and Parcival with you and travel until you come to Sarras, where Joseph of Arimathea had his palace. Ride west along the sea coast and you will find Solomon's ship waiting for you.'

'Lord,' said Galahad, 'can they also travel with us, these knights who have ridden here from Gaul and Ireland and Denmark?'

'No' he said. 'I sent my apostles to different places in the world, and I do the same today. Two of you will die in Sarras, but one shall return to tell Arthur and his knights all the things that happened to you.'

Then he blessed them, saying to Galahad:

'One of your tasks is to heal the Wounded King, and the land laid waste because of him. So before you leave, take blood that has dripped from the spear and spread it on his body. Then you will restore him.'

After that they saw him no more. It seemed like a vision yet it could not have been, because the spear lay on the silver table, dripping into the silver bowl.

Galahad took blood from the container and spread it on the hands and feet of the sick man. No sooner had he done so than the old king's wound was healed. His strength flowed back into his body and he sat up, praising God in a loud voice. He looked like a man half his age. Indeed he looked no older than his son, King Pelles.

Next day he left his bed and declared that he was leaving Carbonek for good. He demanded clothing fit for a poor man and swept aside his son's pleas to give more thought to his decision. He would lead a life of thanksgiving and prayer, he told him. He knew of a priory of White monks who would welcome him. And indeed he left the castle on foot, settled in the priory where he outlived all his children, and became known in later years as a good and holy man.

All the twelve knights remained before the Grail praying for God's protection; and at dawn a voice came to them, bidding the nine foreign knights go home:

'My friends,' it said, 'go now where providence directs you, and where you can work for me.'

They listened gravely and replied together 'Blessed are you, Lord our God, for calling us your friends. That word alone has justified our journey.'

The Meeting Place

Then they went down into the courtyard, armed themselves and took their horses, Galahad, Parcival and Bors staying with them to the last moment. They spoke warmly to each other, and when the time of parting came were deeply moved.

Galahad spoke the final words:

'Friends and brothers,' he said, 'I ask God to bless you all, and should any of you come to King Arthur's court on your journeying I beg that you will give my dearest love to my father Lancelot and to the knights who are our brothers.'

They gave their promise and they rode away.

Galahad, Parcival and Bors now took farewell of King Pelles, his son and the niece who lived with him in Carbonek. They were sad to see Galahad go, but happy for King Pellam. They kissed the travellers goodbye while all the knights and the people of Carbonek gathered in the courtyard to watch them go.

As they rode back into the Waste Land Parcival said:

'Oh! Look around you at the land!'

They could hardly believe what they saw. The streams were full of water; green leaves were growing on the trees, and the grass beneath their horses' hooves was green and full of flowers. Everywhere they saw birds and heard them singing among the trees.

'You have healed the Wounded King,' said Bors, 'and the earth has been healed with him.'

For three days they rode westwards along sunken roads and ancient forest tracks. Miles before they reached it they could hear the boom of the sea as it beat against the rocks, grinding the cliffs away. On the fourth day they saw Solomon's ship below them, and the cliff path gradually led them down to a shingle beach littered with rocks and boulders. All along the sea's edge oystercatchers were feeding, calling loudly as they ran back and forth in the water.

The ship's sails and rigging were exactly as they had been before, unmarked by time or weather, and the timbers still bore the same warnings. Yet as they went closer, leaving the horses on the shingle, Galahad immediately realised that Solomon's ship had changed.

'Look at the table' he cried, 'the silver table!'

They were overjoyed. There was the square silver table from Carbonek firmly secured, and on it the Grail hidden from their sight by the familiar silken covering.

'It will be with us to the journey's end' said Bors. 'We are its guardians now.'

They all went into the ship, leaving their horses. There was only a small breath of wind but gradually it grew in strength so that the big white sails filled and the ship was carried towards the open sea.

They sailed for weeks. The ship seemed to have a life of its own, responding to winds and waves, riding out storms, pausing when the northern fogs came down so that they could barely see one another.

'I wish we knew where we were going,' said Parcival. 'We seem to be sailing to the edge of the world. I wish we knew where Sarras is. Do you know, Bors?'

'Not I,' said Bors, 'but it must be somewhere towards Jerusalem. It is where Joseph of Arimathea lived and where the Grail came from, and where we shall find Dindrane.'

Solomon's ship took them close to many rocky stacks and steep cliffs where the colonies of birds amazed them, and the deafening cries that greeted their arrival. Sometimes they saw islands in the distance, and occasionally they arrived at little coves or inlets where they would have been only too glad to land but they dared not. Thus they came close to the Saints' Island which all of them had heard about. It was a grassy hump of land, housing a colony of austere hermits; a blessed place where no one was ever ill and no one died before he reached a hundred years of age. It was a place of pilgrimage, and Parcival had once met a group of pilgrims making their way home from the Saints' Island, each one carrying a bunch of the holy sea-thrift that grew there.

They saw many different birds on their voyage but mostly kittiwakes that flew quite close to them, seeming to follow them.

Parcival gained confidence from these wandering birds. He told the others: 'Birds are made mostly of air; everyone knows that. Otherwise, how could they fly? Birds are lighter than the wind and they know things hidden from us. They know where land is. They must know where Sarras is; maybe they will lead us there.'

'It's true that we can learn from birds' said Bors. 'Maybe from trees as well.' And he told them about the grey bird he had seen flying around the dead tree where her nest was built.

'When I got closer, I looked into the nest' he said. 'It was full of young chicks but every one of them was dead. Then the mother bird came to the nest and settled herself among them. She pecked herself with her beak so that the blood ran over the chicks. I couldn't believe what I saw: they all became alive again. They got to their feet, flexed their wings and looked around them. But presently the mother bird died among them from the blood she lost.

'After this I knew that the bird and the chicks were telling me something but I couldn't think what it could be. Later on I asked a White monk. He said the bird was showing me how Jesus gave us back our life. By myself I would never have known that.'

'Dindrane would have known' said Galahad, 'for the Holy Spirit taught her all she knew.'

They lost track of time as the ship sailed on. Occasionally they caught a gleam from far inland of burning furze and bracken. Now and then the sound of a warning bell carried over the water; and once in the middle of the night they heard the sound of voices, a low strange singing which came from a great rock a mile or so away. The sound filled them with dread.

'It must be the voice of demons' said Parcival.

The Meeting Place

Bors and Galahad thought it could be the voices of drowned sailors, souls from the other world; but none of them knew what the singing could be. At intervals all through the night, the voices rose and fell.

With the coming of dawn there was silence. The ship was now quite near the rock and they could see a great colony of seals crowded together on its ledges. The knights stared at them bewildered, and suddenly the seals plunged deep into the sea.

'What can they be?' asked Galahad.

Neither he nor Parcival had ever heard of seals, much less seen them at such close quarters. Only Bors had once seen seals and all he knew was what people said about them.

'They are really men and women' he told the others, 'people under a spell. They can change their shape; they can leave their skins behind and become men and women again.'

'They have eyes like people' said Galahad, staring at them. 'They look into your face as people do.'

Bors said 'Sometimes they leave the sea and go to live with Christian men and women, marry them and bring up children. But they always want to go back to the sea, and one day they will take their children and go to live in caves deep in the ocean.'

They were silent, examining the seals now reappearing, every one, from the depths. They lost their fear, marvelling at the strange creatures God had put into the world

'What could they have been singing?' Parcival wanted to know. 'Do you think they were giving us a message?'

Bors had no answer but Galahad said 'I believe they were wishing us godspeed to Sarras.'

He might have been right because for the whole of that day and the next the seals followed them, their dark curious heads coming quite close to the ship.

Now the winter was changing into spring, and still the ship sailed on. No matter how fast their passage, they seemed no closer to their goal.

Parcival grew impatient. Bors never complained and seemed ready to accept their endless journey, just as he had accepted travelling by land and sea on Arthur's campaigns. Galahad fell into silences when he would sit alone, staring across the sea at the white wake of the ship. Parcival wondered if he was praying, for occasionally he caught the sound of words, but he hesitated to ask.

One night the sea was calm, the ship barely moving. Overhead, the sky was very clear.

'Look up at the stars' said Parcival. 'When I was in Caerleon, the astronomers told me that the distance between us and the stars is too great to understand. For if one of us wanted to reach them and we rode thirty miles a day, it would be eight thousand years before we came to the nearest one! Well, how many miles are we from Sarras?'

'We aren't going to the stars' said Galahad, 'but to Sarras where the Grail belongs. We have a different journey, with no milestones.'

Many days later they imagined they saw land far ahead, and a good helping wind took them towards the east.

Now Parcival was sure he heard Galahad pray, and he asked what he was saying. He himself could recite only the prayers taught him by Ashfleur, his mother:

'You must say the Our Father and the angel's greeting to Mary' she had said, and these were all he knew.

Galahad told him: 'When we were all at Camelot that Whitsun, the Grail was shown to us but it was hidden. In Carbonek we saw it plainly. One day in Sarras we may look into its depths. That is what I pray for.'

'But what will you see there?' asked Parcival.

'I cannot tell you' he answered. 'I think it will be darkness. Some light is too bright to look at, for me or you or anyone.'

This left Parcival sad at heart and puzzled, and from then onwards he knew the pain of not understanding what he longed to know.

At last they saw land close to them. Solomon's ship took them swiftly, and before long they sailed into a well-built harbour. They looked about them hungrily. The whole place was full of light and shadows, trees full of fruit, and blossom growing everywhere. Men and women in strange bright clothing moved among the trees and the buildings, and children played by the waterside.

'Is this Sarras?' Galahad said, staring round him. He could not take his eyes off the trees. It was months since any of them had seen a green plant.

Bors said 'Surely it is. This must be the end of our journey.'

CHAPTER 10

In the Eye of Sun

On reaching Sarras the knights take over a fortified tower and make a shrine for the Grail. Before long the king of Sarras imprisons them as spies. When the king dies a year later, a series of circumstances force Galahad to replace him as ruler, despite all his protests; and this role brings evergrowing burdens and pressures.

One morning, at daybreak all three go to pray before the Grail. To their surprise they find another figure there, Josephus, the bishop they had last seen in Carbonek. He calls Galahad forward to look into the depths of the Grail vessel. What Galahad saw neither Bors nor Parcival ever knew, but Galahad's life ends with that vision.

Sarras was much more than a port. It was the capital city of King Estorause, last in a long line of powerful despotic kings. His kingdom stretched from the sea coast far inland where its olive groves and green irrigated fields gave way to sand and stony desert.

In Solomon's ship the three knights stood riveted by what they saw: the painted houses, pink and yellow, rising on the hills behind the harbour, the white towers tall among the buildings.

The harbour itself was full of activity and human voices. Small craft were unloading baskets of glittering fish, selling them on the spot, the fishermen's shouts reinforced by the beating drums. Dockers unloaded great bales of cotton and wool from files of donkeys, while other men swung the bales into the holds of coastal ships tied up at the harbour-side. Over all this flew flocks of screaming birds fighting for the fish-scraps.

Bors and Galahad stared silently, totally absorbed by the scene before them. Not so Parcival. Suddenly he gave a great cry of amazement.

'The ship!' he shouted. 'Look in the water! It's Dindrane!'

Had he been able to swim, he would have jumped into the sea, for at that moment he saw his sister's ship sail in and rest beside them.

Galahad and Bors were dumbfounded but Parcival kept jumping up and down, crying 'She has kept her promise! I knew she would keep her promise!'

While they were still marvelling at this and staring down at Dindrane, they heard her old familiar voice. 'Leave your ship' she said, 'and take the silver table and the Grail vessel. Carry them between you and go to the tower where Joseph of Arimathea lived, and where his son Josephus was the first Christian bishop.'

People gathered in curiosity as the three men began the task of moving the table, carrying it up the quayside through the fish-sellers. It was an almost impossible task. Galahad and Parcival each took a corner, while Bors supported the rest of the weight and did his best to keep the table level, but soon they had to pause. Then Galahad noticed a beggar sitting by a fish stall, his crutches lying beside him.

'Friend!' he called out to him. 'Help us with this burden.'

'Are you mad?' said the beggar. 'Look at these crutches? It's ten years since I walked a step.'

But Galahad urged him, saying 'Stand up and you'll find you can walk again.'

The beggar looked undecided, then he made a move to get up, and suddenly he regained his old familiar strength. He was struck with amazement, and he ran willingly enough to Bors to share the burden with him. As he came, he kept shouting 'I can walk! I've been healed!'

When they heard this, his friends came running up to him. The beggar had been a fisherman until his accident, and he was well-known in the harbour.

'What's happened?' they asked. 'Who's healed you?'

'The young knight' he told them, 'this one beside me.'

His friends looked accusingly at Galahad and the other two.

'How did he do it? Who is he?' they asked.

'I don't know' the beggar said. 'All I know is that I can walk.'

And he began to shout aloud with such effect that the street soon filled with curious bystanders who followed them.

The beggar now led them all into the city through a labyrinth of dark lanes enclosed by high walls. He paused before a gate which opened on to a court of sunlight and shadows and sparkling cascades of water. In the centre was a sturdy round tower made of white stones, shining in the sun.

The crowd fell back because there was no room for them all in the garden. So only Bors, Galahad, Parcival and the fisherman made their way carefully inside, along a stone path flanked by delicate stone arches beside which springs of water had been channelled to flow among the flowers.

They carried the silver table into the tower where the door stood open, and set it down in an empty room. The walls were entirely white, striped with shadows from the metal grilles on the windows.

'This tower is called the holy palace' said their guide. 'At least, that's what the Christians called it when they ruled here. One of their great men lived here once. They say that these walls used to have figures of Christian holy men painted on them. Now they have all been painted out by order of the king.'

'This must have been the home of Joseph of Arimathea' said Galahad. 'This is where we were told to go.'

Bors was examining the thick walls and the defensive windows.

'It's a good secure place' he said.

So they decided at once to take the tower for themselves, and to create a shrine for the Grail.

Their immediate task was to retrieve Dindrane's body from her ship. With the help of the beggar and a couple of his friends, they buried her in the garden near a group of quince trees now covering the ground with their white petals.

'This is a fit place for Dindrane' said Galahad. 'It's like the garden of Paradise'

As they saw more of the city in the next days, they were amazed by the strangeness of it all: the painted houses, the storks nesting on the rooftops, the tall date-palms, the white roses that grew everywhere; and by the ever-present flocks of doves that settled beside granaries and taverns, which no one ever hunted or harmed.

The beggar began to grow more curious about these new friends of his.

'How did you find your way here?' he asked. 'How did you hear about Sarras, since you come from so far away?'

'We found our way here because God guided us.' said Galahad. 'The seas and the winds obey him.'

'Well' said the beggar, 'we believe that, too. We say that every wind that blows has to go first to Jerusalem for God to bless it. After that it blows wherever he sends it. So you are certainly here with his blessing.'

He also spoke secretly to the three, warning them to stay within the tower, not to draw attention to themselves.

'There is a lot of talk about you already. There aren't many Christian people in Sarras. There's a little group of holy men who live together at the very edge of the city, but they have been there for a long time and people are used to them. They aren't used to you.'

All this was true enough, and before long King Estorause sent secret agents to keep watch on them.

From the white tower the knights could look down on to the busy harbour and the shipping and yet be unobserved; and it was not long after the fisherman's warning that Bors suddenly realised that Dindrane's burial ship was no longer there. What is more, Solomon's ship had also vanished, as secretly as she had sailed away from him so many centuries ago.

Bors was startled and he called the other two.

'Where can Solomon's ship have sailed this time?'

Parcival made light of it.

'She'll come back one day as secretly as she left, and take us back to Camelot.'

At that Bors felt a sudden piercing longing for the grey seas and skies, the green moors and forests of home.

'No' Galahad said, 'we shan't see her again. She has fulfilled her purpose.'

When King Estorause heard that the strange white ship had vanished from the harbour, he was enraged and sent a posse of armed men to the tower with orders to bring the three before him.

They were led into his palace through hall after hall lined with panels of ivory, until they reached the Judging Place where the king sat on a throne of ivory and silver, his archivist and secretaries behind him.

He said 'You three are spies from the West.'

They denied this.

'Your accomplices have stolen that white ship from the harbour and sailed away with it.'

Again they denied it.

'You have come here to spy on our defences, to steal our trade.'

'We are no merchants' said Bors, 'nor spies, nor thieves.'

'Then why have you come here?' the king demanded. 'Why have you taken over the White Tower that once belonged to the Christians? Who gave you permission to settle in here? And what is this silver table I have heard about? Are you magicians who use it for witchcraft?'

He turned his hard seamed face to Bors.

'You are the oldest, the leader. Answer me these questions.'

'I will answer you' said Bors, 'though I am not the leader.'

Then he told the king why they had set out to search for the Grail, and that they were now its appointed guardians in Sarras.

Estorause listened intently. His secretaries and the archivist wrote with great speed as Bors spoke, and then presented their writings to the king. He studied them with concentration and presently he gave his verdict.

'You are either fools or very clever spies plotting against our kingdom' he said. 'This story of yours is clearly false, and I shall see that you regret this voyage. You will all be imprisoned in the palace until I shall decide otherwise. My will is absolute and no one can overrule it. Make sure that this decision is recorded' he said to the archivist, and tossed his book back to him.

As soon as Estorause had seen fetters riveted round their ankles, the three were locked into a crumbling stone cell in the palace wall. Then the king sent soldiers to the White Tower with orders to bring him the silver table, the Grail and anything else of value. To his fury, they came back empty-handed. Both table and vessel had vanished clean away.

The king returned angrily to the cell to question the prisoners. They could give him no answer. They had no knowledge of where the Grail had gone, nor who had stolen it, and no matter how he threatened they were not to be moved. Finally he left them, convinced that they spoke the truth.

Meanwhile the three discussed uneasily among themselves, wondering if they were failing in their mission, hoping fervently that the Grail might show itself to them and set their minds at rest. And in fact from time to time while they were in prison they would become aware of its presence, and this gave them strength.

Their cell was small, hot and dusty, partly below ground with a narrow horizontal window lined with iron bars. At least they could see across a great sun-dried area and sometimes watch the king's archers at practice, or a parade of horses, and they could hear the shouts of the mounted guard responsible for the king's safety, who patrolled his palace day and night.

No one spoke to them and no one visited them except a silent soldier who brought bread and water once a day. Each morning, when the soldier had gone, Parcival scratched a mark on the floor with a sliver of stone he had found in the cell, and thus he calculated the length of their imprisonment. When six months had passed, he sighed and said:

'God can do anything. He made the relics of St. Non work miracles. Didn't he make St. David's spring flow with milk instead of water when people were starving? Didn't he make a field of barley ripen overnight to help them? Why shouldn't he make the walls of this palace fall down one night, and send us a ship?'

But the walls stood firm, and another six months went by.

Then one night, when it was dark – for they were never given a lantern – and all they could hear was the wind blowing dust into the cell, Galahad suddenly sat up on his bed and asked the others:

'Do you remember what the king said when he imprisoned us?'

They remembered it only too well.

Galahad went on. 'Did he say it was God's will? No, he said it was his will to put us here for the rest of our lives. He said that no one can overrule his will. He said nothing about God's will. Now since he believes he is stronger than God, I believe God will free us one of these days, and then the king will see who holds the power.'

Then he went back to sleep in the straw.

Galahad proved to be a good prophet. Some weeks later they were taken from their cell and their fetters struck off. They were then led deep into the palace to a bathing room where clear water flowed out of great cisterns, and where they could wash away the dirt of their imprisonment. Palace officials shaved off their beards, cut their hair and provided them with new clothes. A sense of urgency and anxiety pervaded the palace. They felt it strongly but no one gave any explanation until they arrived at the office of the king's archivist. He was friendly enough and had them sit down while he explained why they had been summoned. King Estorause had fallen ill. He could neither eat nor sleep, and had lain in his bed for many weeks.

'His doctors have done all they can. The whole college of medicine is resident in the palace with all their skills; yet the king gets worse, not better.'

He looked Bors straight in the face and said again:

'He gets worse. He will not live long, so he ordered me to bring you to him.'

Bors said quickly 'We are no doctors.'

The archivist almost smiled and said:

'Have no fear on that score. Sarras has no need of Western doctors; they know little or nothing of true medicine. Any skills they have, they learned from us. No, you are brought here for another purpose.'

Then he told them about the efforts made by the king's Council to raise the sick man's spirits by calling in singers, storytellers, poets and musicians to his bedside.

'None of that helped much, so in the end they called me in as chief archivist. Every day I have been trying to hearten him by reading from the court records about his glorious victories in battle, the fame of his army, the beauty of the Sarras horses, the magnificent buildings he has raised, and his constant encouragement of astronomy and mathematics and all the sciences. And when I came to his reputation as a law-giver and a righteous judge, he suddenly remembered you and how he put you all in prison a year ago.'

He hesitated, lowered his voice, and then he said:

'The king is near to death, and he knows it. He is repenting his errors, recompensing those he has treated unjustly. That is why he summoned you.'

The archivist led them to the king's bedside. It was a brief visit, for Estorause could barely speak and they had to bend low to hear him as he murmured:

'I did you an injustice. Forgive me.'

After that he became inarticulate and half conscious. The archivist waited for the reaction of his victims. He watched them kneel down beside the king, heard them forgive him, each in his own words, each with the greatest gravity and conviction. He was deeply impressed.

Two days later the king died and Bors, Galahad and Parcival were soon reinstated in the tower; and to their great joy they found the Grail on its silver table just as they had last seen it.

During the king's illness, his Council had begun to look for a successor. One after another was proposed but there was always some reason to reject him. The situation grew unstable and dangerous, until the leader of the Council prevailed on the other members to abide by the decision of a man they all revered as a prophet. This was an elderly cleric who lived out in the desert, serving at the shrine where one of the early rulers of Sarras was buried. So they despatched a group of local priests and soldiers to escort this man to the palace. He came readily and listened to the arguments. When everyone had had his fill of words, the prophet went out into one of the palace gardens where he prayed all that night until the next evening.

The Council members were still waiting for his word. No one had dared to leave before his return. With no preamble he said:

'I have been shown who is to rule this kingdom. When I burnt the myrrh, the smoke rose up in a cloud and showed me the misty shapes of three men. Two were young, one was older. They were all armed like men from the West. I burned more incense, then two of the figures faded and one became clear. I knew then that the youngest of these three must be the King of Sarras.'

At this, fresh arguments broke out which were only quelled by a great commanding voice that rang through the room:

'Obey the prophet! Make Galahad the king. Let him be your leader and protector.'

So the whole Council went together to the tower with their request. Galahad totally rejected it with all the eloquence he had. They pressed him hard and still he refused, with Bors and Parcival adding every protest they could think of. But in the end the Council prevailed, threatening all three of them with death unless Galahad agreed.

And now his way of life was quite changed. Bors and Parcival could go on living in the tower but Galahad, like Estorause and all the Sarras kings before him, was immured within the palace; and wherever he went, day and night, the royal guard surrounded him.

He asked Bors and Parcival to build a shrine for the Grail. At his instructions, they called woodmen to bring the finest acacia wood, and carpenters to make a chest like the ark that was made in the days of King Solomon. Galahad sent gold from the Sarras treasury and employed goldsmiths to line the ark inside and out; and he put the Grail vessel inside the ark. He also got smiths to make a golden candlestick with three branches springing each side from the central stem, so that seven lights could burn day and night.

Every day Galahad rose early for a brief visit to the tower. His new duties and responsibilities left him no time for more. Every day he found the antechambers of the palace filled with claimants: judges and soldiers, merchants and criminals, friends and foes. Each day these people varied but the numbers never grew less. These sessions went on until nightfall, and sometimes well into the night. Often he had no time to eat; often he was too exhausted.

And he had also to receive deputations from other kings and rulers; meet merchants seeking trading advantages; visit the buildings being erected; inspect the army and the famous horse displays; advise on the financial state of Sarras; and act as judge in cases of violence, murder, fraud and treachery. He felt for all these people who sought him whether for advice, for revenge, for redress, for favourable judgements. He listened to them, he took action where he could, but he bent under the endless pressure.

Only occasionally could he take time for private meetings with Bors and Parcival, and find peace in the tower with them. When they did meet and discuss their experiences and concerns, it engendered in them a humbling recognition that Sarras had skills and learning and sciences far beyond anything they had ever met in the West. In Sarras books were common, the palace had libraries of books. The yellow-painted houses, often three storeys high, were set among groves of apricots and skillfully-tended gardens. Cartographers, surgeons, makers of surgical instruments were all treated with honour, as were armourers, painters and musicians. Galahad himself had visited the schools of medicine, mathematics and astronomy, and had been overawed by what he found there. Even Bors was humbled by the thin nimble horses of Sarras, so unlike the heavier horses he was used to. In his whole life as a knight of the greatest kingdom in the West, he had never seen archers who could shoot from horseback, nor horses trained to gallop and stop dead in their stride at a command, to stay motionless while riders flung themselves on and off the saddle, nor horses that fought with hooves and teeth should their rider be unhorsed in an encounter. He never tired of watching the parades, the horse-training and the great horse-market which brought buyers from miles away. He sighed in the face of all this knowledge and skill.

'We have nothing like this at home' he said regretfully, almost in disbelief at what he witnessed.

As for Galahad, his awareness of the sophistication and wisdom in Sarras made his task of ruling and advising increasingly burdensome.

'Oh God' he said, 'have I not been long enough in this place with all its troubles?'

Then he heard a voice speaking from the noisy streets of Sarras. It said 'Do not think that the God you seek is one who sits in the high heavens. He has come on to this earth and lives in your midst, and shows himself among you.'

Each morning Bors and Parcival would light the candles on the seven-branched candlestick and pray before the Grail. Galahad would join them when he could. He had now ruled exactly one year in Sarras, and the city was full of green flags and pennants to mark the anniversary.

On that particular morning Galahad got up very early and made his way unseen to the tower, where he found Bors and Parcival waiting for him in the garden. When they entered the chapel they halted in surprise. Beside the silver table stood a man wearing the robes of a bishop. He was evidently expecting them for he had lighted the candles already, and he held an open book in his hands.

He smiled and said 'Come forward, friends.'

They gathered round him, wondering but no longer fearful to advance and watch him at the altar. When he reached the central part of the Mass, the bishop uncovered the Grail. He said:

'Many good knights and good Christians have prayed to see what you see now but they never saw it. And a few have been given a glimpse for no more than the blink of an eye.'

None of them understood that he was speaking of Lancelot when he said that.

He put the vessel back on the table and turned to Galahad saying:

'This is what you set your heart on, this is what you have sought. So come now and look into the depths of it.'

Galahad took the vessel in his hands. He brought it close to his face and looked into it. He began to tremble as another kind of awareness took over his human faculties. Yet he was able to cry out with a strong voice 'I thank you, Lord, you have let me see what I longed for. It is beyond any word or thought.'

When they had all received the eucharistic bread, the bishop turned again to Galahad saying: 'Do you know who I am?'

Galahad shook his head, and the bishop said:
'You have forgotten. You first saw me in Carbonek on the day you travelled through the Waste Land. The shield you carry is the shield I marked with the red cross and gave to Mordrain to keep for you. I am Josephus. My father Joseph came here from Arimathea, and I lived in this very tower.'

He paused and put the Grail vessel back on the silver table. He smiled and put his hands on Galahad's shoulders.

'We are alike, you and I' he said. 'We have both been shown the secret of the Grail. And so the Lord has sent me to be your companion, for you are going to him this very day.'

Then Galahad said goodbye. Turning to Parcival and Bors, he kissed them both, embraced them, and he said to Bors:

'When you see my father again, give him my dearest love and tell him to remember all we spoke about when we sailed the seas with Dindrane.'

He spoke to Parcival, too, and then he knelt down before the Grail, resting his arms on the silver table. Bors and Parcival went to his side. He was silent for a time. Then his arms fell and he slid, falling face down on to the mosaic floor. He died dazzled by a brightness no human being could endure. It would have been easier to look into the eye of the sun than into the face of God.

Then Bors and Parcival saw the Grail's last miracle in Sarras. Josephus vanished, and a human hand appeared above the table. It took up the Grail vessel and carried it into the heights of the tower, and then beyond their vision.

★

When Bors and Parcival saw Galahad lying dead they could not hold back their grief. Indeed they came close to despair at the loss of their friend and brother. They were not the only ones bereaved. The people of Sarras and its surrounding countryside mourned him as well, for Galahad had done much for them in his brief rule.

Immediately Bors despatched a messenger to bring one of the Christian hermits to the tower. In the past year he and Parcival had grown to know them well. With the hermit present, they buried Galahad beside Dindrane in what he himself had called the Paradise Garden

Then Bors and Parcival collected their few possessions from the tower and locked the door, leaving the silver table empty and unused. They rode away with the hermit to the Christian settlement in the sandy hill country. They admired these men whose life was hard and restricted, and who prayed and worked together rather like the monks they had known at home. Bors and Parcival soon joined in the daily programme and grew used to the rhythm of their work and prayer.

Parcival questioned these hermits.
'What did Galahad see before he died?'
'Only he could tell you that' the hermit said.
'He talked about darkness and light. What did he mean?'

The hermit said 'You must know that God is both light and darkness. He is hidden and open. We cannot see him as he is; he lives where ideas and understanding cannot penetrate. No one can tell you what Galahad saw.'

When they had lived with the hermits for some weeks, Parcival made up his mind to join them, and Bors did nothing to deter him. He was too loyal to leave his friend. He stayed on with him but he remained the knight he had been for so long. And now he began to think he ought to go back to Camelot and to King Arthur, but he remained in the settlement until Parcival died there some twelve months later.

They buried Parcival on the left side of Dindrane, while Galahad lay at her right. All the brotherhood took Parcival to his grave, and the garden was filled with people from the city.

When they had put the last of the earth on Parcival's grave, one of the hermits turned to Bors who was weeping and said to him:

'Friend, do not grieve because Galahad, Parcival and Dindrane are all buried in a strange land. If they died far from their friends and families, remember that they are not far from God who is their resurrection.'

Later, he asked Bors about his future plans, urging him to stay in Sarras with the brothers.

'You could do great good in this country' he told him. 'Have you not heard about the prophecies of the White monk Joachim in Spain?'

Bors knew nothing of him. The hermit told him:

'This is a holy man, a true prophet, and many are listening to him. He says that we shall soon move into the third age of the world. The first age was when God the Father revealed himself, and the second when the Lord Jesus came; and now in the third age the Holy Spirit is coming to awaken us and renew us. He will speak directly to each of us so that we shall understand without the need of books or teachers. Consider what you could do if you stayed with us in this land where the Lord is neither known nor honoured.'

'I believe I should go back to King Arthur' Bors said. 'someone must tell him that Galahad found the Grail.'

The hermit tried to persuade him. He said: 'This new age will be like broad daylight compared with dawn. It will be like high summer compared with winter.'

But Bors would not listen. His mind was made up, and his only wish now was for his own country. As soon as he could, he took a horse and his old armour and rode south to the port of Acre where he found a ship due to sail to Venice within a fortnight.

He bought food for himself and grain for the horse, a mattress and bedding, and arranged his passage in a three-masted galley, slow and heavy. He had the company of sixty knights and merchants, together with their servants and horses.

It was a long tedious journey, and the threat of pirates and fierce winds caused the ship to seek harbour time after time. The ship called at Rhodes and at various of the small Greek islands; and it took Bors ninety days to reach Venice.

There he joined up with a party of pilgrims and made his way across Italy and Germany until one day he came to Calais.

Once in Britain, he rode swiftly to Camelot.

By now his armour was rusted and battered, his surcoat and shield faded by sun and wind so that the white star on his blue shield was no more than a shadow of itself.

At Camelot the few knights who had come back from the quest received him with disbelief, with stupefaction. He had been away for years and they had all believed him dead, but once they got over their amazement they began a great celebration throughout the castle, from the cellar to the battlements.

King Arthur and Guinevere spoke with him privately, and each exclaimed and lamented as he answered their questions. They knew something of the quest since Lancelot had told them what he knew, but their knowledge was incomplete.

Finally Bors said to Lancelot:

'Your son Galahad sent his dearest love to you; and after you, to the King and all the knights. And he asked you to remember what you spoke about when you sailed the seas together.'

'I trust his prayers will strengthen me' said Lancelot. Then later he took Bors by the arm and said to him secretly:

'I swear that I will never fail you in the years to come. Count on me, I will be your faithful friend so long as we both live.'

Arthur asked Bors whether Parcival had sent any messages or greetings. 'I always said he would make a good knight' he said. 'I knew it the first time I saw him.'

But Bors could not remember. 'He told me that he was afraid of the sea. He never dreamed he'd have to go so far away.'

'And his sister Dindrane?'

'No' Bors said. 'Dindrane sent no greetings, but a woman in Scotland is alive to this day because Dindrane gave her life back to her.'

Arthur could never hear enough of what had happened. He decided that Bors should tell the story all over again to a scribe in the court who could write it down. When the book was completed, he said, he would donate it to the library in Salisbury Cathedral for safe keeping.

It took Bors a long time to remember all the details and the order of events. He met regularly with the scribe, and as autumn passed into winter a great frost and cold fell on the land. The stars began to fall from the sky; not single stars but in such numbers that no one could count them. Fear grew over the whole land. Then the ice melted but the tides began to sweep far inland, sinking ships and flooding the fields.

'What can it mean?' Bors asked himself uneasily, as he went on telling his story. Many others asked themselves the same question, Arthur in particular. At last the king said to himself 'This must be what Merlin foresaw. These are the signs of destruction and the last days.'

A Kind of Travelling

The Winter World

Merlin has long since left Arthur's court and the king's star is fading. The old company of knights who searched for the Grail has been decimated and a different spirit is abroad, spreading jealousy and revenge. Lancelot, Guinevere, Bors and Arthur all become its targets. Arthur's nephew Mordred brings about the final destruction of the fellowship at the battle of Camlann in Cornwall.

After this slaughter only a handful of knights is left alive, Lancelot and Bors among them. They form a tiny company, a faithful community, whom Bors will later lead back again to Sarras. Bors is the last survivor of the quest, the one who travels furthest of them all.

It was not long before Bors realised that the Camelot he had returned to was a changed place. Many knights, old friends and companions were absent now, and Arthur had new men close to him. After such a long absence Lancelot was no longer his right hand. That honour now belonged to Arthur's nephew Gawain; the first knight to propose the quest, and the first to give it up. And Gawain had allies in his brothers Agravain and Mordred, men who had since arrived in Camelot with their two youngest brothers Gareth and Gaheris. Bors was deeply disturbed by the influence exerted by this group; they were a formidable tribe.

Lancelot was unhappy, too. He had come back deeply marked by his quest and his failures; and remembering his solemn promise to the hermit who had encouraged him, he avoided occasions when he would have to be in the queen's company. He spent much of his time with Bors, and their friendship deepened in consequence. He sought for occasion to ride away from Arthur's court, so he took upon himself the causes of various women who thought themselves unjustly treated by the law. Still, in the end his resolution failed and he and Guinevere became lovers as before. And this time there were spies, Mordred and Agravain, who watched them and spread news of their secret meetings.

While Lancelot became increasingly aware of the hostility towards himself and Guinevere, she was blind to it. He tried to warn her, but in vain. Indeed, his warnings simply increased her anger and resentment.

'You have changed' she said accusingly. 'Your love has cooled, you are avoiding me.'

He tried to explain.

'I have kept away because Mordred is spying on us. I have told you that Gawain's brothers would like to denounce me as traitor to King Arthur. This means that you are in danger, too. If I am accused, so will you be. You must believe me, this could mean death for both of us.'

Guinevere broke into a storm of furious weeping.

'This is not true!' she cried. 'You shun me because you prefer those women you are always riding away to visit. Now you are back from that quest, I am nothing to you. I see it clearly. Go to those ladies you have such love for and keep away from me. I forbid you this court from now on.'

Angry and dismayed, Lancelot took himself off to Bors.

'I shall go back to my father's kingdom' he said, but Bors was adamant.

'You and I have known Guinevere for years' he said. 'She is a woman with no patience and she is forever changing her mind. She'll soon forget those angry words and urge you to come back.'

Lancelot was not easily mollified, though Bors eventually dissuaded him.

'Stay here' he said, 'but take yourself off secretly to Sir Brastias, that friend of mine who lives only seven miles from here. Meanwhile I will send you news of any developments.'

So Lancelot stayed with Brastias.

When the Christmas festivities were over, Arthur and the court made plans to ride to London. Lancelot followed them unobserved, and took lodging with a hermit in the woods near Windsor. This was an old crippled man who had been one of King Arthur's knights in the early years of his reign. He had fought in many battles. He had spoken with Merlin and had been present at the marriage of Arthur and Guinevere. Lancelot found him a good companion.

In early spring Bors brought urgent news.

'The queen has been captured!' he cried. 'Meligaunt has kidnapped her!'

Meligaunt was a Scots knight, a close friend of Mordred and of the whole Orkney tribe.

'Guinevere went with her friends into the woods to celebrate the spring' said Bors, 'to bring back willow branches and all the early flowers. She had only ten men with her, and not a sword among them.'

"Where is she now?' Lancelot demanded.

'Meligaunt has them all in his courtyard, and most of the men are wounded. The queen says she will protect them and will never set foot inside his castle; and she will stay with the wounded men. We know all this because a boy escaped and brought us the news.'

'How many men are with you?'

'Twenty.'

Without hesitation Lancelot took his armour, pulled himself into the saddle, and the group rode away immediately, with the old hermit calling out blessings on them.

The Winter World

Within the next two hours they had swept down on Meligaunt's castle, freed the captives, consoled the queen and cheered the wounded men lying in the courtyard. True to her word, Guinevere had refused to leave them, so she and they were taken in farm-carts from the castle to Arthur's court.

While this was taking place Meligaunt, who had hidden himself from Lancelot, secretly made his way to Mordred's quarters where he found all the Orkney brothers assembled.

They were quick to respond to his news.

Agravain said 'The king must be told that Lancelot has come here plotting to see Queen Guinevere again.'

Mordred said 'We should be ashamed to do nothing when we all know that Lancelot and the queen are lovers, traitors to King Arthur. Someone should tell him.'

Gawain disagreed. 'It is none of our business.'

Agravain contradicted him. 'I am ready to tell the king.'

'Not with my agreement!' cried Gawain fiercely. 'It will cause open war between us and Lancelot. It will do great damage to the whole brotherhood.'

He left them in anger, and hardly had he gone than the king himself appeared, to ask the knights what they had been discussing.

Agravain did not hesitate but told him plainly: 'We were talking about Lancelot. We are your nephews, the sons of your sister, and we cannot see you betrayed by Lancelot. You must be the only one in the court who doesn't know that Lancelot and the queen are lovers.'

Arthur's response was calm enough.

'Lancelot has always been the best knight among you' he said. 'He will cope with any accusations you may make. What proof have you of this? Bring me proof, and then I will listen to you and take action. Until then you had better be silent.'

Mordred said 'Tomorrow you go hunting and will be away all day and night. Mark my words, Lancelot will be here in your absence. We shall wait for him and you shall have all the proof you need.'

That night Lancelot sat talking with Bors. As it grew near midnight he got to his feet and said 'Goodnight to you, Bors. I am on my way to speak with the queen.'

'Do not go on any account!' cried Bors. 'I know what Agravain and Mordred are saying. You are in great danger if you visit her tonight.'

'But the queen has sent for me' said Lancelot.

So Bors, heavy-hearted, watched him go.

Lancelot wrapped his woollen cloak round him and secretly made his way through the dark castle to the queen's room.

Hardly had he greeted her and bolted the door when Mordred and Agravain and their followers, all fully armed, gathered at the door shouting:

'Traitor, open the door! You are caught now!'

Lancelot was completely taken by surprise.

'I have only a sword with me' he said to Guinevere. 'Is there any armour here?'

'No' she said. 'No shield nor armour, nothing.' She was trembling with terror.

Meanwhile, the shouting grew louder.

'Open the door! Come out! Show yourself!'

Lancelot wrapped his cloak about his arm and opened the door just wide enough for one man to enter. Agravain rushed forward, sword in hand. Lancelot stepped back and struck him such a blow on the head that he fell down and never moved again.

Quickly bolting the door, Lancelot cried to Guinevere 'Come, help me with this' as he began to unbuckle the dead man's armour. He put it on and took up his sword again.

'Traitor!' the knights kept shouting. They had now brought a great billet of wood and were battering the door.

Lancelot paused and turned to the terrified Guinevere.

'If I am killed' he told her, 'go to Bors. He will help you; he is our truest friend.'

Then all at once he flung open the door and stormed into their midst, fighting with such ferocity and strength that before long all his enemies except Mordred lay dead or dying on the ground. And Mordred fled away, weeping for his wounded arm.

Lancelot's victory brought him no sense of triumph. He turned to Guinevere, distressed and weary.

'God help me' he said. 'After these deaths I shall never be seen by anyone except as the king's enemy and rival.'

He kissed the queen and quickly made his way to where Bors was quartered in the castle. Bors was surrounded by a group of knights all hostile to the Orkney brothers. Lancelot told them what had happened, and Bors listened sombrely.

He said 'This may well mean death for the queen, and for you as well, as a traitor.'

'There must be some escape!' cried Lancelot. 'If Guinevere is condemned we can rescue her. I shall take her with me to Northumbria until the king's anger passes and she can return.' So they set to and made plans for this eventuality.

Meanwhile Mordred sought out the king, who had now returned from hunting. Displaying his blood-stained arm and hand, Mordred shouted vehemently that Arthur had been betrayed. 'We have all the proof we need. He was with the queen last night, as I told you he would be.'

'Jesus, mercy!' cried Arthur. 'God, spare us!'

'He has killed ten knights; he has killed your nephew Agravain; and he has wounded me.'

'Did you truly find him with the queen?'

'We did. They have both betrayed you.'

'My God, this is a bitter blow' said Arthur. 'It will split our company, for some will side with Lancelot; but if the queen is guilty she must pay the price.'

All that day Arthur sat alone, his door bolted, refusing to discuss the situation with anyone and rejecting the queen's frantic pleas to speak with him. He prayed for guidance, he wept at his role of judge, he tried in vain to find some way out.

Next day he called the knights together and as their law-giver and lord gave his decision: The queen should suffer death by fire.

'I appoint Gawain to oversee the execution' he said.

But Gawain protested, and many of the other knights rallied to him.

'I will have no part in this' said Gawain, 'and I will not remain here to see it. The queen should not be burned.'

After this resistance Arthur gave the same command to Gawain's brothers Gareth and Gaheris, young newly-made knights only recently arrived from Orkney. They dared not refuse but, young though they were, they protested that they would take no active part, would carry no weapons, would be no more than onlookers. 'Sir, we want no part in the queen's death.'

Finally Arthur gave the responsibility to Mordred who took it with alacrity.

The queen was now a prisoner confined to her room. Her women took away her crown, her shoes, her jewels and her robes of blue and crimson. They dressed her in a long linen shift. Then the king's chaplain put a cross into her hands and set about hearing her confession.

Meanwhile in the courtyard the executioner was stacking wood, tar and kindling around an iron stake fixed into the ground.

From her room in the tower the queen could hear the men's voices. She did not dare look from the window, and turned her attention to the priest who had begun to intone the penitential psalms:

O LORD, DO NOT REBUKE ME IN YOUR ANGER; DO NOT
PUNISH ME, LORD, IN YOUR RAGE.

She could not understand the Latin and she hoped that the words would give her strength. Presently the priest turned towards the door, and Guinevere's ladies gathered round her.

'Follow me' he said.

Gareth and Gaheris stood near the stake unarmed, unwilling spectators sorrowing for the queen. As the door of the castle opened, they saw the sad slow procession: first Mordred and a dozen knights; then the priest with his book; then Guinevere, barefooted on the hard ground; and after her all her devoted women, every one of them in tears.

The executioner tied Guinevere to the iron stake and set fire to the wood. Soon tongues of flame licked round her feet and she was hidden within billowing clouds of smoke.

The priest drew back and continued with his prayer:

IF YOU, O LORD, SHOULD MARK OUR GUILT,
LORD, WHO WOULD SURVIVE?
BUT WITH YOU IS FOUND FORGIVENESS.

Suddenly his voice was lost in a tremendous shouting as Lancelot, Bors and some twenty armed knights rode furiously into the courtyard. Amid the smoke, the shouts, the clatter and clashing of arms, Lancelot did not recognise Gaheris and Gareth, and in the confusion he cut them down.

While knight fought knight with swords and maces, Lancelot snatched Guinevere from the flames and rode away with her. Bors and the other knights trampled Mordred down, unhorsed and wounded his men and left them lying dead in the courtyard.

When Arthur heard of the queen's escape and the death of so many of his knights, especially of Gaheris and Gareth, he could not hide his dismay.

'Do not tell Gawain about his brothers' he cried. 'It will cause yet more harm; it will mean war between us and Lancelot.'

He wept and grieved.

'My heart was never so heavy as it is at this moment' he said, 'and I grieve for Lancelot and for my knights more than for Guinevere. For I might find another queen, but I could never again find such a fellowship.'

Next day when Gawain returned he found the court full of the news. Secretly he was glad that Guinevere had escaped.

They told him: 'Ten knights were killed when she was rescued.'

'Where are my brothers?' he asked.

'They were killed beside the gallows.'

He was appalled. 'But they had no swords!' he cried. 'What criminal would kill them, two young knights, two boys?'

'They were killed by Lancelot.'

Gawain would still not believe it but when eyewitnesses swore to the truth of it he fell to the ground in terrible distress. Then he ran to the king and the two of them grieved and wept together the whole night long.

Next morning Gawain said to Arthur: 'I will have revenge on Lancelot. I will follow him wherever he goes, no matter how long it takes. It will be my death or his. I swear this by God.'

Escorted by Bors and his men Lancelot rode with Guinevere to the coast of Northumbria, to Bamborough where he had his castle. Here he defended her successfully against the onslaughts of the army Gawain persuaded the king to dispatch. Indeed Gawain now made himself the real leader of the army, and though the king was present he found it impossible to enforce his wishes against Gawain's fury for revenge.

Nevertheless the hostilities were inconclusive. Neither side could vanquish the other and after Bors and Gawain had each been wounded in single combat the fighting dwindled.

News of this dispute spread throughout the kingdom and eventually came to the ears of the Pope in Rome. As the Bishop of Rochester happened to be in Rome as a pilgrim, the Pope soon sent him back as his emissary to King Arthur. In the most solemn terms the Pope deplored the scandal of violence between Christian men, and he commanded Lancelot and Arthur to make peace with each other. He also demanded that Guinevere should return to Arthur and be restored as queen.

The bishop handed this document to King Arthur. Indicating the great iron seal which adorned it he said: 'Unless you accept this decree the whole land will be put under an interdict. Then every church will close, and every monastery. You will have no priests for christenings or weddings; and after death you will all be buried out in the fields like animals.'

Arthur was glad to accept. He wanted Lancelot as his friend again.

The bishop then took the Pope's letter to Lancelot whose acceptance was as wholehearted as the king's had been.

'Now the queen will be safe again' he said. 'Tell King Arthur that Guinevere will return to him eight days from now, and I thank God that I can take her back to him.'

He kept his word and when Arthur had received his wife again he said to Lancelot:

'Alas that there has been enmity between us. Let us have peace now. You are still dearer to me than any of my knights.'

Lancelot would have responded to this but Gawain shouted:

'The king may do as he wishes but I will never make peace with you; for you killed my brothers when they were defenceless.'

Lancelot offered to make amends. He said he would walk barefoot from Carlisle to Kent, and at each ten miles of the walk he would give money for a hermitage to be built, where a hermit could pray for the two young men.

Gawain scorned his offer.

'Leave the queen' he said as though he had the king's authority, 'and leave this place as fast as you can. If the Pope had not commanded your protection I would kill you now.'

So Lancelot spoke to Guinevere in the hearing of them all.

'I see that I must leave this fellowship for good, and so I beg you to pray for me; and if you need me, send me word.'

He kissed her and said to all the assembly:

'You know that I am and always will be the queen's true friend.'

Then he and Bors rode away with his knights, and many people wept.

Arthur watched him go, filled with dismay and disappointment. He knew that he could do nothing to placate Gawain. 'With all this present sorrow' he said within himself, 'I know that the year will not rise with me. My time is running out.' He rode back to Camelot from Northumbria, a great and gloomy journey.

Later in the autumn news came to Gawain that Lancelot, Bors and their group of knights had left Bamborough, had taken themselves to Cardiff and sailed away to the kingdom of Benwick where Lancelot's father was king. By this time they had established themselves, each settled on land granted them by the king.

When he heard this, Gawain's rage broke out again. Time after time he urged the king to invade Benwick to harass these rebels. Arthur resisted but in the end it was Gawain who prevailed. The king called for the building of a new fleet of ships. He sent out proclamations all over the country and gathered a huge army. Then he made Gawain's brother Mordred regent and put Queen Guinevere under his personal protection.

Finally after much delay he and the army sailed away from Cardiff to France, where they set out for Benwick, laying waste the land, destroying crops, polluting wells, and burning down all the villages they passed through. Then they laid siege to Lancelot's castle.

Week after week passed, full of inconclusive sorties and encounters. Within the castle Lancelot and his friends disputed whether to stay within their defences or to ride against the besieging troops. 'We should not stay here like rats in a hole' some said. Yet others said that more lives would be lost if they attacked.

Regularly, Gawain rode out to challenge Lancelot and to taunt him for cowardice and murder.

Then one day in the early morning, as Bors watched from the tower, he saw to his amazement that Arthur's troops had begun to retreat. Spies soon reported that the army had left behind them all their stores, cattle, baggage and prisoners in their tremendous haste to get back to the ships that had brought them. Neither Bors nor Lancelot could imagine what this meant.

It was only when a solitary knight, riding under a flag of truce, arrived at the castle that they began to understand.

'I have come from King Arthur' the knight told Lancelot and Bors. 'Gawain has written a letter for you. It is urgent. It is an appeal for help in the disaster that has fallen on us.'

'What disaster?' they asked him.

Then the messenger told them a tale of treachery, greed and malice. Mordred, ambitious and as envious of Arthur as he had been of Lancelot, had spread rumours of Arthur's death in battle and had declared himself king. Guinevere had fled from him and taken refuge in the Tower of London. The Archbishop of Canterbury had excommunicated Mordred, and had been threatened with death.

The messenger told them:

'When king Arthur heard this, he took the army back at once. His ships sailed to Dover where the king found Mordred's troops waiting for him. They fought all day long on the sea shore and many knights were killed.'

'Gawain was wounded' he went on. 'I saw him. He was lying in a piece of wreckage at the water's edge and he was at the point of death; yet he found strength to write to you to ask your help, to ask forgiveness.'

When they heard these tidings Bors and Lancelot did not waste an hour. The moment they could get ship they sailed with all their army to Dover. Their arrival was too late. The wreckage of battle still littered the seashore, and there was no sign of Arthur's army.

The news they received was shattering:

'The king is dead, Mordred is dead. They fought all day long and thousands of men are still lying on the battlefield. Gawain died, too, from his wounds and we buried him here in Dover Castle.'

In the midst of all this grief Lancelot asked for news of Guinevere. Nobody knew where she was, but rumour had it that she had also fled from London into the West country on hearing of the king's death.

From that moment Lancelot determined to find the queen. He put Bors in charge of the army, saying 'Wait two weeks for my return. If you don't see me by then, take to the ships and go back to Benwick.'

Bors tried to deter him. When that failed he proposed to go with him, but Lancelot would not listen, riding away without a word.

In the days to come Lancelot found towns and villages mourning for men lost in the fighting, and trying to make good the ravages of war, since many of the villages lay in ruins. He rode for days, stopping to enquire at any monastery or convent he came across. So he went as far north as the Forest of Dean, as far west as the Brendan Hills, through Frome and Shaftesbury. One day he found himself near the Cistercian nunnery in Wareham by the sea. Here he received the first good news; the abbess told him that Guinevere had passed that way, and had gone on to take refuge with the Benedictine nuns in Amesbury. And there Lancelot found her.

He begged her to come away with him to Benwick and the safety of his father's kingdom. Guinevere listened, stricken with astonishment at seeing him, weeping silently, holding herself within the protection of her women. She listened to all he said but she was quite resolute. When he fell silent, she turned towards these women and said:

'My sisters, my friends, it is through me and this man standing here that King Arthur has been killed; and not only the king but the flower of all his knights. It is because of our love that the kingdom has been destroyed. This thought is always with me. I repent of all I did, and I ask you to forgive me.'

He was amazed to hear her speak with such determination. He tried again to persuade her, but she said:

'Lancelot, my life is changed. I am resolved to stay here in this place, to pray with these sisters so that I may see the face of Christ at my life's end. I beg you to go away, find yourself a wife and be happy with her.'

He refused. 'That I will never do' he said. 'You tell me that your life has changed, that now you seek God with all your heart. Then I swear that I will do the same. It is what I should have done when I went in search of the Grail; then I might have seen what Galahad saw.'

In this way they parted, all her women and the nuns weeping as they took the queen back to her room while Lancelot rode away.

He thought 'I must find some hermit or some good man who will accept me.' He let his horse go where it would. The pathway led through a gorge, oaks and mossy outcrops on one side, sheer rock on the other. Gradually the track gave way to wooded slopes, and they in turn became a sort of heathland cut through by narrow, fast-flowing streams, with here and there a bridge of moorstone.

After an exhausting day, he found a small chapel with a house built on to it, set in the middle of a garden which had been wrested out of the moorland. He was surprised at the remoteness of it. He slid wearily off his horse and went into the chapel.

Suddenly his spirits soared; he came face to face with Bors who had disobeyed his orders and gone in search of him. They embraced one another in disbelief, joy and amazement on their faces.

As they emerged from the church Lancelot met two more familiar faces: the knight Bedevere and the old Archbishop of Canterbury who had fled from Mordred's tyranny and established himself in this chapel as a sort of hermit.

It was only now that Bors and Lancelot heard details of the battle between Arthur's and Mordred's forces, an encounter in which the earth shook under the weight and ferocity of men and horses. The armies fought all day and thousands lay dead on the heathland beside the river.

'Oh, unhappy fated day!' Arthur had cried. And fated it was. The armies struggled all through the summer night until Arthur had no more than two knights left alive with him: the brothers Lucan and Bedevere.

It was Bedevere himself who told all this to Lancelot and Bors. He said:

'In the end Mordred had no man left alive except himself. We saw him hanging onto a staff, for he was exhausted and his horse was killed. Then the king saw him, and cried out for his spear. We tried to restrain him. "Let him alone" I said, "he is doomed anyway."

"Doomed or not" the king said, "he will not escape me now." With that, he took his spear in both hands and rushed at Mordred. You know that his spear is ten feet long. He struck Mordred, and the spear-blade came ten inches out of Mordred's back. Yet in spite of this, Mordred forced himself closer to the king and cut through his helmet. They both fell together, and Mordred died as he fell.'

Bedevere told them how he and Lucan his brother had carried Arthur to the bank of the river which flowed by the battlefield. Lucan was badly wounded, a great gash across his chest. The effort of carrying the king was too much for him and he died under the trees.

Lancelot could not restrain his grief. Tears ran down his face.

'This is the worst news I have ever heard!' he cried. 'so many deaths!'

Then he asked 'Where is King Arthur buried?'

Bedevere said 'The king was nearly dead; he was silent. A barge came down the river to where he lay. There were women in the barge, all veiled in black. They cried and mourned, and took the king away with them. There was no more I could do then, so I buried Lucan and made my way from the battlefield; and one day, just like you, I found this place.'

It was certainly a miracle that they had met again. They asked the Archbishop if they could stay with him, and he was glad enough to find disciples. So far as they knew, Lancelot, Bors and Bedevere were the only survivors of the Round Table. Yet as the months passed, two more found their way to the hermitage; young nephews of Lancelot: Bleoberis and Blamor.

These five lived simply together, almost as Bors and Parcival had lived in Sarras after Galahad's death. They took over the care of the chapel, cultivated the garden, prayed together, and protected the people of the countryside.

In this way six years passed, and one night Lancelot dreamed that Guinevere was calling him. With Bors and the rest of the knights, he set out at once to walk to Amesbury, only to find that she had died peacefully during their journey.

The nuns told him 'Our sister Queen Guinevere knew from the Lord that she would not see you again, and she told us that you should bury her in Glastonbury.'

This they did with all the ceremony at their disposal, with prayers and candles and vigils at her tomb.

From that time onwards Lancelot's will to live dwindled, his energy flagged, and they knew he would soon leave them. He wanted nothing, he said, except to be buried in Northumberland. So on his death the whole group put his body on a horse-drawn bier and travelled more than two weeks to Bamborough, where they buried him in sight of the sea.

There was no life for them in Northumbria now, nor indeed in any part of the kingdom, for Arthur and Lancelot were both dead and a new ruler held the power. Bedevere and the other two turned to Bors for counsel, recognising his experience; for he had been Lancelot's truest friend and follower. He had taken part in the quest of the Grail, and he had travelled as far away as Sarras and had returned in safety.

'Tell us what to do' they said.

So Bors led them back to the East, to Sarras. They found a ship in Venice and some nine weeks later landed near Jerusalem. After a time, they were accepted as colleagues by the knights who lived beside the Temple and, with their agreement, helped to keep the highways safe from robbers, protecting pilgrims from attacks by local bandits. In this service Bedevere and the two younger men Blamor and Bleoberis each lost their lives one Eastertide, and Bors buried them outside the walls of the city.

Then Bors himself was killed, fighting with the Temple Knights in a battle that littered the rocky ground with fallen men and horses. The Temple Knights were bound by their rule never to leave the battlefield while their standard was still flying, never to desert it while any comrade of theirs remained alive. The Knights' black and white standard was still flying bravely, but near it lay Bors' broken shield with its faded silver star.

A Kind of Travelling

★

There was no one living now who had ever seen the Grail; no witness to the search men had made to find it, no one to tell where it had been taken once it had been withdrawn from Joseph's tower in Sarras.

Yet far away from Sarras the Grail stronghold was still standing on the wildest headland of Wales, to the east the forest, to the west the open seas; the force of the tides grinding away the cliffs, the boom of the waves audible far inland.

The land that had been desolate and wasted had long recovered its growth and greenness; and as time passed, the trees encroached closer to the castle walls and hid them. Indeed some of the outer walls began to crumble, though the chapel remained exactly as Lancelot, Galahad, Parcival and Bors had known it.

Sometimes travellers passed that way, but very few. It was as if Carbonek was still meant to be hidden from human sight; and the occasional travellers who did come close wondered what lay behind the walls, but did not venture to come closer.

Yet one day two travellers from far away heard about the Grail Castle and eventually found their way there, into its inner places and its chapel. The people living near Carbonek remembered these travellers, for when they eventually emerged from the place they were changed people.

'What has happened?' they asked them. 'What did you find inside the castle? What has changed you? What did you see there?'

The travellers answered: 'Go where we have been and you will find the answer.'

Bibliography

Le Morte D'Arthur, Sir Thomas Mallory. Edited: Janet Cowen. Penguin 1969

The Quest of the Holy Grail. Translated, with an introduction by P. M. Matarasso. Penguin 1969

Arthurian Romances, Chrétien de Troyes. Translated, with an introduction and notes by D. D. R. Owen. Everyman/Dent Revised 1993

High History of the Holy Grail. Translated from the Old French by Sebastian Evans. James Clarke & Co, Cambridge

The Journey Through Wales; The Description of Wales, Gerald of Wales. Translated with an introduction by Lewis Thorpe. Penguin 1978

The History of the Kings of Britain, Geoffrey of Monmouth. Translated with an introduction by Lewis Thorpe. Penguin 1966

The Mabinogion, Revised Edition. Translated by Gwyn Jones & Thomas Jones. Everyman/Dent 1989

The Plantagenet Chronicles. General Editor: Elizabeth Hallam. Tiger Books International PLC 1995

Parzival, Woolfram von Eschenbach. Translated by A. T. Hatto. Penguin 1980

The Medieval Warhorse: from Byzantium to the Crusades. Ann Hyland with a Foreward by Michael Prestwich. Grange Books 1994

Arms & Armour of the Medieval Knight. David Edge & John Miles Paddock. Saturn Books 1996

The Making of the Middle Ages, R. W. Southern. Arrow/Hutchinson 1953

The Mass of the Roman Rite, J. A. Jungman. Benziger, New York 1950

The Shape of the Liturgy, Dom Gregory Dix. Dacre Press, Westminster 1954

History of the Mass, Robert Cabié. Translated by Lawrence Johnson. The Pastoral Press, Washington DC 1990

The Grail Society

The Grail Society is a group of men and women dedicated to God and centred on Christ. Basically Roman Catholic, it includes people of many different Christian traditions, people who believe in creating community, empowering others, and valuing each person wherever they may be in their spiritual journey. Grail members try to be aware of God's presence in the natural world, in society, and in the people they encounter.

The Grail Society comprises several groups: a community of lay women (the author Philippa Craig belongs to this group), married couples, single women living in their own environment, young adults, associates and a family network. The Grail Centre, a large house set in ten acres of grounds and situated on the outskirts of London, is the home base for the society. Here some of the Grail people live, leading workshops and seminars aimed at bringing together creativity, healing and faith. A number of hermitages in the grounds offer space for people under stress or seeking spiritual renewal to stay for short periods. The Centre is at Waxwell Lane, Pinner, and may be contacted by email at *waxwell@compuserve.com*